ADERSHIP *for the*

NEXT GENERATION *of* **EXECUTIVES**

The E SUITE

Tina Kuhn & Neal Frick

GREENLEAF
BOOK GROUP PRESS

Published by Greenleaf Book Group Press
Austin, Texas
www.gbgpress.com

Distributed by Greenleaf Book Group

For ordering information or special discounts for bulk purchases, please contact Greenleaf Book Group at PO Box 91869, Austin, TX 78709, 512.891.6100.

Design and composition by Greenleaf Book Group
Cover design by Greenleaf Book Group
Cover illustration used under license from
©Shutterstock.com/Devita ayu silvianingtyas

Publisher's Cataloging-in-Publication data is available.

Print ISBN: 978-1-62634-994-0

eBook ISBN: 978-1-62634-995-7

Part of the Tree Neutral® program, which offsets the number of trees consumed in the production and printing of this book by taking proactive steps, such as planting trees in direct proportion to the number of trees used: www.treeneutral.com

Printed in the United States of America on acid-free paper

22 23 24 25 26 27   10 9 8 7 6 5 4 3 2 1

First Edition

To Leslie Lewis, for her sage advice and delicious wine, her dining room table for bringing us together, and the dachshunds—Bruiser and Ranger—for keeping us entertained.

CONTENTS

Contents

Why Is Empathy Important in the Workplace?

We started working together when we were hired as leaders in a business that needed to undergo a transformation due to market loss. The company required a complete strategic shift to build up market share and new offerings. The new strategy encompassed changes to all aspects of the organization: building a robust business development pipeline, expanding into a significant number of new customers, creating intellectual property, creating business discriminators, and strengthening the business processes, tools, and infrastructure.

As we worked through the transformation, we realized we had different styles of leadership that balanced each other. Tina liked fast decisions. Neal was more thoughtful and liked to take a day or two to think through all aspects of the problem. We both quickly learned to appreciate the other's style and learned to respect each other's opinions but also pushed and challenged each other. During the first year in the transformation process, we started to have regular retrospectives on how we could do better individually and as a team.

Conversations about balancing employees' needs against the organizational needs increasingly became front and center. As our discourse continued, we found ourselves discussing the practical application of empathy in business.

Our understanding of empathy began to evolve as we explored the following questions: How can we better serve our employees without compromising the organization's success? What should drive our decision making? If we want to build a people-first culture, where do we start? It occurred to us that empathy was something completely different from sympathy and compassion. Empathy is the ability to understand and relate to an individual's emotional state, motivations, and needs while reserving judgment and remaining neutral.

As we began to make decisions based on empathy, we saw a positive impact on the business. While our decisions didn't always align with what people wanted, we could address our reasons for making those decision in terms they could hear and understand. These positive changes became the driving force behind writing this book. We had found a low-cost, high-return solution that we believe is of critical importance for every organization. This strategy is especially crucial now, when the statistics around employee engagement, attrition, and customer satisfaction are startling.

On average, 50 percent of people in the United States are unhappy in their current position and are looking for a new job at any given time.[1] Fewer than 40 percent of employees feel that they are engaged with their employers.[2] The job market is in a constant state of high attrition, and productivity is at an all-time low.[3]

Simultaneously, customer dissatisfaction is at an all-time high. People who interact with your organization can post their complaints and concerns online for potential customers to see. Rating sites like Angi have become ubiquitous, and a poor customer experience can have long-term negative consequences. These negative impressions carry weight offline as well, as reflected in the White House Office of Consumer Affairs study showing that a dissatisfied customer tells, on average, twelve people about their bad experience. Dissatisfying customer service is an experience that can't even be undercut by low prices, since customers are reportedly almost four times more likely to move to a competitor over a service-related issue compared to a price-related issue.[4]

How do you combat the challenging statistics facing the modern workforce and make your organization stand out for its personnel? How can you effectively maintain an engaged and loyal customer base? In a post-COVID world, how do you adjust to the paradigm of remote work and support your employees while still maintaining business continuity?

Rene Schuster, former CEO of Telefonica Germany, puts it this way: "Empathy is not a soft nurturing value but a hard commercial tool that every business needs as part of their DNA."[5] Schuster implemented an organization-wide empathy training program that led to an increase in customer satisfaction of 6 percent within six weeks.

Empathy is a low-cost solution to many of the challenges facing today's organizations. In this book, we will offer practical suggestions for how to structure an organization, develop a culture of empathy, and manage individuals and teams for a productive and happy workforce.

The first part, Organizational Strength through Empathy, dives into how to build an organization with empathy, how to develop high-performance teams, and how to leverage empathy when approaching issues of diversity and inclusion.

The second part, Managing and Leading with Empathy, presents four different management styles and a method for determining which is the most appropriate style for each situation. It also unpacks how to embody empathetic leadership while communicating virtually and in person, during confrontations with employees and customers, and when guiding organizations through difficult, uncertain times.

The third part, Growing a Business through Empathetic Leadership, discusses organic growth, hiring, marketing, and sales. The strategies outlined in this section form a concrete guidebook to increasing market share through innovative and empathetic strategies.

The tools and information within this book will deepen your understanding of the importance of empathetic business practices, show you how to apply them successfully, and drive business growth in ways that support the needs of both customers and employees.

Understanding how to create significant change within an organization starts with one question: What is empathy?

The word "empathy" was first used by the psychologist Edward Bradford Titchener in 1908. It was modeled on the German *einfühlung*, which means "in feeling." The term was originally coined to describe the theory that art appreciation is dependent upon the viewer's ability to project a version of themselves onto the artwork. The idea was that to understand a piece of art, you must be able to see yourself reflected in it in some way. In its original definition, empathy had nothing to do with interpersonal relationships; instead, it was used to describe the act of projecting yourself and your emotions into the world around you.[6]

The concept of empathy as we have come to know it did not emerge until the late 1940s, when the neuroscientist Rosalind Dymond Cartwright began conducting tests on what she called "interpersonal empathy." During this study, she refined the earlier understanding of empathy, defining it as the interpersonal connections fostered by the ability to see yourself in another person's position. In 1955, *Reader's Digest* defined empathy as "the ability to appreciate the other person's feelings without yourself becoming so emotionally involved that your judgment is affected."[7]

The definition has evolved over time, growing to encompass many facets of the human experience. In each of the three parts of this book, we will explore the definition of empathy as it relates to the themes of the chapters therein.

Empathy is the ability to understand and relate to an individual's emotional state, motivations, and needs while reserving judgment and remaining neutral. What sets empathy apart from emotions such as sympathy and compassion is the way it allows us to understand and relate to other people while maintaining a neutral emotional state—which also makes empathy a powerful tool in a professional work setting.

Since business is built on relationships, an empathetic approach to leadership will help foster and develop essential relationships with customers, clients, and the public. To better understand how it works in business, we'll start by looking at the biological underpinnings of empathy.

LOOKING THROUGH THE MIRROR

Not so long ago in the early 1990s, a team of Italian researchers discovered a new kind of brain cell called "mirror neurons" in the anterior cingulate cortex—the region of the brain involved in higher-level brain functions such as attention allocation, reward anticipation, decision making, ethics, and morality.[8] Mirror neurons are "a type of brain cell that respond equally when we perform an action and when we witness someone else perform the same action."[9]

Think about watching someone stub their toe or get a paper cut. Did you wince? Although you might not physically feel their pain, witnessing someone injure themselves can cause your body to experience a similar—albeit much less intense—reaction. According to the neuroscientist V. S. Ramachandran, this is because between 10 percent and 20 percent of the neurons associated with pain are mirror neurons. As Ramachandran summarized for *Greater Good Magazine*:

> So these [mirror] neurons are probably involved in empathy for pain. If I really and truly empathize with your pain, I need to experience it myself. That's what the mirror neurons are doing, allowing me to empathize with your

pain—saying, in effect, that person is experiencing the same agony and excruciating pain as you would if somebody were to poke you with a needle directly. That's the basis of all empathy.[10]

And because no one leaves their mirror neurons at home when they go to work, if someone witnesses a colleague or employee in pain or experiencing a difficult time in the workplace, they will have a physical and emotional response of their own. Clearly, empathy exists in the workplace whether we choose to acknowledge it or not, but let's explore the benefits of leveraging empathy in business.

Introduction

Low Cost, High Return

Empathy is the ability to understand and relate to an individual's emotional state, motivations, and needs while reserving judgment and remaining neutral.

THE VALUE OF EMPATHY IN BUSINESS

Many leaders view empathy as an intangible quality and find it prohibitively difficult to assign a monetary value to it. While there is no simple formula to determine the direct return on empathy, the increase in sales, customer engagement, and employee productivity are measurable.

The modern business climate is incredibly competitive, and to stay competitive there must be a constant drive for innovation and productivity. This mindset pushes leaders toward a fast-paced, high-stress environment with expectations for monumental growth. This approach can lead to productivity, but it is not sustainable. Often, when trying to grow a business, leaders sacrifice interpersonal relationships for the sake of expediency, which is shortsighted, especially as the employee-employer paradigm shifts and people in the workforce expect better treatment.

In a survey conducted by Deloitte, a management consulting firm, younger generations are looking to employers to create diverse, engaged, and employee-centric organizations:

> Viewpoints of millennials and Gen Zs will be critical when creating a new and better normal. Employers should promote dialogue . . . listen to their concerns and strive to understand why certain issues really matter to them. Leaders also should ask for input . . . help employees prepare for the future . . . and better enable people to realize both their personal and professional ambitions.[1]

Employers are starting to understand the value of relationships and the importance of empathy in building their businesses and connecting people. Over the past few years, research shows CEOs are increasingly embracing the need for empathy in the workplace. Conversely, the number of employees who believe they work for an empathetic employer is decreasing.[2] Why is that? As younger generations enter the workforce in greater numbers, the bar for empathetic and ethical leadership rises. The expectations of Millennial (b. 1981–1996) and Gen Z (b. 1997–2012) employees are outpacing the rate at which employers are making changes to their organizations' cultures.

There is a perception in the business community that empathy is a "touchy-feely" emotion and a weak managerial approach. However, it is impossible to deny that businesses run on relationships—between managers and employees, salespeople and customers, and even between the business and the public. Social dynamics have changed, and employees are increasingly focused on work/life balance.

There is a tangible benefit to understanding the individual and specific needs of people within an organization as well as their customers. This approach builds trust and strengthens relationships, allowing for a more collaborative and productive environment. Outside the organization, this approach yields a deeper understanding of the customer base and a stronger connection between the customer and the organization.

EMPATHY AFFECTS PRODUCTIVITY

Most people spend a quarter of their life at work. They have complex and often combative relationships with their careers and they enter an organization eager to succeed. If they are treated well and their needs are met, they will become emotionally invested and their productivity will improve. If they are treated poorly, they will become disengaged. This will reduce their productivity over time and may result in them leaving the organization altogether.

For those employees who remain, their willingness to go above and beyond is closely tied to their engagement with the organization. Discretionary effort, the additional effort above and beyond the minimum that a person could give, is impacted by how their management treats them. In 2020, 74 percent of employees indicated that they would be willing to work longer hours for an empathetic employer, compared to 60 percent in 2017 through 2019.[3] Empathy and compassion are increasingly becoming must-have attributes for an organization to entice someone to work for them.

PART I

....

ORGANIZATIONAL STRENGTH THROUGH EMPATHY

Empathy is understanding what motivates
and inspires people to greatness.

P eople are the cornerstone of any organization. Motivating and engaging them is critical to ensure the success of a business. People work best when they understand the leader's vision and feel connected to their managers. Leadership sets the tone for the organization; positive, engaged, and empathetic leaders inspire people to do their best work.

Building and developing high-performance teams takes empathetic leadership and the ability to see individual strengths and weaknesses. An empathetic leader puts people in positions where they can be successful based on their unique contributions. A team focused on specific, achievable goals who feels strong connections to their management and one another will accomplish great things.

Finally, diversity and inclusion within organizations is a foundation of a healthy and robust organization. Diversity of thought creates space for unique and inventive solutions to problems. Addressing your own fears and biases toward people of different backgrounds and embracing diversity makes the organization stronger.

Chapter 1

Building Strong Organizations

The heart of every organization is the people. Regardless of the processes, procedures, organizational structure, or type of work, it is critical to focus on the people to build a strong organization.

The Businessolver 2020 State of Workplace Empathy study found "93% of employees say that when their employer recognizes their professional accomplishments, it boosts their overall work productivity." In addition, "82% of CEOs believe a company's financial performance is tied to empathy."[1]

> **"82% of CEOs believe a company's financial performance is tied to empathy."**

People are the most motivated and engaged when they feel they are a critical part of the organization's success; when they are contributing to something that will benefit society as a whole; when they can grow and learn and try new things; and when their leaders are supporting them. Employees give the most at work if they feel like they are part of something greater than themselves.

To build a strong organization, everyone in the organization should understand how everyone else's task helps the common goal. This cross-role understanding can be achieved in several ways, including staff meetings where roles are discussed, a written document discussing each role in the organization, and presentations by each team to others on their day-to-day tasks.

Every role should directly support the organization's goals and mission. The leader and team members must be able to articulate why each role is important, and if they can't, then the leader needs to determine if that role is really needed.

Building a strong organization of any type requires a focus on the people that make up the organization. Being people-oriented does not mean giving overly high salaries or benefits or doing harm to the organization by keeping people who are not performing well. Leaders within a people-oriented organization focus on keeping employees engaged, motivated, and focused on the goals of the business.

It is a fallacy to think an organization cannot be strong financially if the organization is people-oriented. Engaged personnel are far more productive and willing to work harder for the organization, thus saving the organization money. Personnel who are happy and motivated make fewer mistakes.

Being people-oriented not only translates to a better culture but also helps customer satisfaction. Think about it: When you encounter a surly employee at a business, do you want to engage with them again even if they have a superior product? On the flip side, when you encounter an engaging, happy person, they draw you in and you are more likely to return to that business.

A LEADER'S EMOTIONS FLOW DOWN

"Attitudes are contagious—make yours worth catching."

—Anonymous

There is a strong tie between a leader's emotions and their team's emotions. If a leader is positive and energetic, the team will reflect that. If the leader puts out negative emotions, their negativity will permeate throughout the organization.

The following story shows how a change from a negative-energy leader to a positive one can impact a team.

New Boss

Betty, Mike, and Yolanda sat nervously in the conference room with their heads down and fidgeting. Today they were meeting their new boss: Bill. He walked in smiling and made it a point to shake each person's hand and say how happy he was to have them on his team. Betty sat a little straighter and said it was nice to meet him. Their

continued

old boss had criticized them constantly, so they learned to keep their heads down, ignore his ranting, and just do their work.

In contrast, Bill respectfully asked each of them what their job responsibilities were and listened to each answer without interrupting. Bill kept his body open and his hands casually folded on the table. Bill then asked what they thought could be done to make their job better. Mike almost blurted out "be nice to us," before finally offering up an idea that Bill considered a real process improvement.

The next day, Bill told the staff about Mike's idea, gave Mike credit for it, and said it would be implemented immediately. Bill came by several times a day to see Betty, Mike, and Yolanda and praised them for the great job they were doing. All three started offering ways to save money and make the office more efficient, blossoming under Bill's praise.

The Lesson: Leaders are far more responsible for their team's emotions than they realize. They must exude positive energy—but they must also be genuine, so their nonverbal communication matches their words. Otherwise, employees will respond to the body language and discount any words being said.

WHAT HELPS PEOPLE ENGAGE?

In a world that is becoming more automated, impersonal, and online, workplace communication and connections are very important. The COVID-19 pandemic accelerated remote working and business automation, changing many organizations' business models permanently.

The personal connections created at work through day-to-day casual contact are greatly diminished with remote work. Employee engagement must be more deliberate and planned with a remote workforce.

Here, we'll explore four ways for employees to develop a strong emotional connection to their workplaces, all of which an empathetic leader can leverage in service of a stronger organization.

Understanding the Vision and Goals of the Organization

All employees must have a clear sense of the values of the organization. They not only need to understand the organization's vision and goals, but also their personal role in achieving those goals. The organization's vision should be the team's road map to success.

Let's look at an example where an employee did not know their organization's vision and the goals.

Customer Service Is Number One

Joe was thirty-four years old, making a living by stocking shelves at a local grocery store. He was grateful for the job, but he'd been there only a week before he knew it had no future. It was the kind of job where he could be replaced by someone else at any time. Even so, Joe arrived on time every day and did what he was asked to do.

One morning, while he was stocking up the cereal, a harried woman came in with a crying two-year-old girl. Joe asked if there was anything he could help her find that morning. She thrust her shopping list at Joe and thanked him while she tried to console her

continued

11

daughter. Joe went around the store, selecting the five items on the customer's list before bringing them back to her, all the while thinking he would be fired because he was not stocking the shelves. The woman thanked him profusely and went to pay. Joe quickly finished what he was doing and ran into the back to get more goods to continue stocking.

As he was lifting a box of toilet paper up onto a shelf, Sheila, the very strict store manager, came down the aisle. She obviously wanted to talk to him. Sigh—Joe really needed this job. He had an explanation ready to go when Sheila smiled and thanked him for his conscientiousness with the harried mother. Sheila predicted that Joe had created a very loyal customer by taking extra time to help her.

Realizing he wasn't being fired, Joe relaxed and told Sheila he liked helping people. She said that was a good thing, explaining that the only way the store could compete with the larger grocery chains was with superior customer service. Any time a customer needed help, Sheila explained, Joe should stop whatever he was doing and help them.

Sheila walked away from their conversation thoughtful, realizing she had never impressed upon her employees that customer service was her number one goal and that every single employee had something to contribute toward that goal.

The Lesson: Knowing why their jobs are important to the organization helps employees feel important and needed and helps them prioritize their time and effort effectively. How can employees make the right decisions if they don't know the end goal?

Feeling They Matter to the Organization

People feel they matter if their ideas are listened to, and if the leadership acknowledges and recognizes their work and accomplishments. While formal reward programs are fabulous, the little things are just as important: the acknowledgment of a significant event, kudos for a job well done, a hello and a smile every day, and a thank-you in the hallway for something they did.

Let's continue exploring Joe in the grocery store to show how listening to an employee makes him feel he matters and how doing so helped streamline the organization.

Joe's Bright Idea

Joe had been working about a month stocking shelves at the grocery store. He went back into the warehouse and found that, once again, the delivery guys had put pallets of canned goods right in front of the items he needed to stock. Frustrated, Joe ended up pushing pallets around and climbing over boxes to get what he needed. The warehouse was so disorganized! He finally got the boxes onto the cart to take to the shelves, but now he was covered with dirt. He brushed off what he could, sighed, and went out into the store. At lunchtime, he noticed Sheila, the store manager, was by herself in the front of the store.

Joe took a deep breath and approached Sheila, asking if he could have a moment of her time. He explained that he'd spent half his day moving boxes to get to stock, and there must be a better way to organize the warehouse so the items that needed stocking every day could be easy accessed. Sheila asked him how he would do it. Joe

continued

quickly explained how he thought the daily stock items could be set aside, even in the small warehouse. Sheila nodded and asked him to show her.

Over the next two days, Sheila, Joe, and the receiving person reorganized the warehouse to make it more efficient. The next Monday, Sheila presented Joe with a $50 gift certificate in front of the whole staff, thanking him for his initiative. Joe felt more pride in his job than he had in a long time and was grateful for Sheila's recognition.

The Lesson: Effective leaders are open to different ideas and perspectives. Soliciting ideas and honestly evaluating each idea without bias is critical for happy personnel. When people see their ideas being implemented in the organization, they feel respected and hence highly engaged. The more the leadership understands the personnel's point of view, the more the decisions will be empathetic and people-centric.

Having a Connection with Managers and Coworkers

It is important in any work environment for the team to connect with each other. It is logical that if someone has friends at work, they do not want that community to dissolve, and so they work harder for the organization. In a workforce with increasingly remote workers deprived of most casual interoffice communication with each other, it is even more important to create ways for managers and coworkers to connect.

Let's look at an example of the importance of connecting with a remote workforce.

Long-Distance Relationships

Carol was a biller in a large corporation. A few months ago, the corporation decided to close the building where she worked and moved everyone remote. They said it would save them a lot of money not having to pay rent and utilities for a large office building in the downtown area. For the most part, Carol was okay with working from home. The commute had been forty-five minutes each way, so she saved a lot of time and gas money not commuting. She also cooked lunch for herself, so she saved a bunch of money by not buying lunch out. However, Carol felt very down and depressed. She missed her coworkers. She missed all of them eating together every day. She missed hearing about their families, and the drama in their lives. She was lonely. Carol's work started to get sloppy as she slumped into a deeper depression. At the end of a Zoom call, one of her coworkers asked how she was doing. She said she was okay but she missed everyone. All the other coworkers chimed in and said they missed her, too. Someone suggested doing a virtual lunch a day or two a week to sit around and chat. Carol smiled and said that would be great. Carol and her four close coworkers started having virtual lunches every Tuesday and Thursday. On Friday, they invited their boss and others to join in a larger virtual lunch. Carol felt happier, and her job performance improved significantly.

The Lesson: People are far more engaged when they feel that they have friends at work. It's essential to strengthen these work connections through informal gatherings where conversations can become more personal. For example, in remote meetings, schedule five to ten minutes of open discussions before meetings start, or have virtual happy hours. For face-to-face teams, eating together in a lunchroom, pot-luck lunches, and after-work gatherings are good ways to strengthen the connections between people.

Being Part of Employee Development Programs

Most people thrive when they are learning new things or see a growth path for themselves. Work with each person to develop a list of skills and knowledge that will help them get to the desired next step in their career. There are a variety of inexpensive ways people can gain job skills.

- **Job shadowing:** Create a buddy system pairing a junior employee with a senior employee. The "buddies" spend time together on a regular basis. It's amazing how much they will learn from each other.

- **Online courses:** Free or inexpensive training material is readily available. For example, LinkedIn Learning has online classes and seminars for free or for a nominal monthly charge, with more than 13,000 courses to choose from.

- **Brown bag lunch-and-learns:** Schedule internal mentors or subject-matter experts to talk to employees during lunchtime.

Typically, this is on the employees' own time so there is no cost to the company.

- **Team member workshops:** Hold workshops so teams can share their wealth of knowledge with each other.

- **Provide a membership for online courses:** Online classes are typically much lower in cost than attending seminars or college classes.

- **Pay for subscriptions to online publications or ebooks:** The online publications help keep employees on top of new trends and technologies.

- **Informal mentoring:** Encourage employees to create mentoring relationships with less-experienced staff.

Let's look at how an informal mentor can help an employee's development and career path.

The Mentor

Marcus had been working as an IT technician for a large organization for more than a year. He liked the job but had ambitions of advancing his career and becoming a network engineer. Marcus researched some training he wanted to take and presented it to his supervisor, who explained that they had no money for the class. Besides, they could not afford for him to take a week off for the training. After their conversation, Marcus started looking for a new job that had career potential.

continued

The next week, Marcus was pulling cables for a new office area when he got talking to one of the network engineers. The network engineer told Marcus where to find the best free training material and said he would answer any questions he had. Marcus was elated and immediately started studying the material on his own time. The network engineer discovered Marcus was a quick learner and talked his boss into petitioning for Marcus to be transferred to the network team as a junior network administrator. Marcus thrived, and in five years he became the network engineer team supervisor. Peer mentoring had saved a great employee from leaving the company, and Marcus put in more effort every day because he felt someone at work really cared about him and his career.

The Lesson: Setting up a mentoring system is also a great way to help employees feel engaged, both for the mentor and protégée. Effective mentoring systems do not have to be formal or expensive. Pairing people together for biweekly or monthly chats can go a long way in keeping people engaged in the organization.

Wrap-up

∙∙

Creating a people-first organization does not have to take a lot of money or time, it just has to be a conscientious focus of the leadership. The following are key aspects of a people-first framework:

- Displaying genuine, positive, and energetic leadership
- Ensuring each person understands the vision and goals of the organization
- Making every person feel like they matter by showing them respect, listening to their ideas without bias, implementing their good ideas, and communicating frequently
- Offering programs that allow personnel to connect with their coworkers and managers
- Offering employee development programs so each person can see a growth path for themselves

Chapter 2

High-Performance Teams

When you think of a great team, what is the first thing that pops into your mind? Maybe your first thought is a team you previously worked with, a handful of passionate people working toward a common goal. Or maybe your college friend group, who always managed to work together to get into some sort of trouble. Maybe you think of the Avengers.

Great teams can be made up of people of varied skill levels, people with diverse backgrounds, and even people who may not entirely get along outside of the situation that brings them together as a group. Empathetic leaders can cultivate certain group characteristics for teams to be more dynamic, efficient, and productive. All effective teams share a few common traits:

- Clarity of purpose
- Strong communication

- Ability to resolve conflict quickly and positively

- Accountability and shared responsibility

- Diversity of thought and background

- Equivalent contribution

- Willingness to support each other and celebrate individual successes

YOUR DREAM TEAM

Leading a team presents a unique set of challenges that can be met effectively and successfully when approached with empathy. Whether you are dealing with an existing team or creating a new one from scratch, there are steps you can take to ensure your new team is more cohesive. This may mean making tough decisions, especially about individuals on the team who are struggling to perform their duties.

When selecting new team members, do so with an empathetic, people-focused approach, using what you know about existing team members' working styles to find the most harmonious fit. There are a few factors that impact how new members will work with and augment an existing team. Some people are individual contributors, effective at staying in their lane and working on tasks to completion. Some are collaborators, able to build consensus and execute on ideas fleshed out by others. Teams are a mix of individual contribution and group work, so pay attention to what roles potential new team members might be suited for to ensure that your team has a balance of members who excel at each kind of task. If a team is made up of only individual contributors, you may find your team members are unable to see the bigger picture and only understand their individual roles. If you have a team built entirely of collaborators, there may be excellent conversations about new and exciting ways of doing business, but there might not be any progress.

> **A study conducted by *Forbes* of more than 200 teams determined that diverse teams make better decisions 87 percent of the time.**

Studies have shown time and again that inclusive and diverse teams are more effective than homogenized teams. A study conducted by *Forbes* of more than 200 teams determined that diverse teams make better decisions 87 percent of the time.[1] Consider the experience mix of your team. Do your team's members have diverse experience, backgrounds, and worldviews? If not, they may have difficulty thinking of new and exciting ideas.

When encountering an existing team, there may be resistance to new ideas due to years of doing things the same way. "We have always done it this way" is a dangerous statement in any organization. In this situation, an agitator may be required, someone to push a team outside their comfort zone and shake things up. The word "agitator" has a negative connotation, but think of it this way: Have you ever worked with someone who frustrated you by challenging your pre-conceptions? Maybe a boss tested you regularly, or a coworker always played devil's advocate. How did you respond to it? If your gut reaction to these memories is negative, take a step back from the emotional reaction and look at it as an outside observer would. How did those challenges impact your work? Did you try different solutions? Did you see things from someone else's perspective? Did the agitation open you up to other ideas or experiences?

Another trait shared by successful teams is the opportunity for members of the team to mentor and develop their peers. No leader can be everywhere at once, and there will be times that a team needs guidance from within. Peer mentorship is when a person has experienced something that their peer has not and is able to help them navigate the situation with gentle and collaborative guidance. Watching who is doing the mentoring on the team will indicate the next generation of leaders within the organization.

When building a team or augmenting it, be sure to consider an individual's ability to work within a group, their experience, and their ability to shake things up. Choose people with diverse backgrounds to add new and interesting perspectives to your team.

EMPATHETIC TEAM LEADERSHIP

The same *Forbes* study that showed the power of a diverse team also revealed that a well-managed team will outperform individual decision makers by 66 percent.[2] Teams thrive when they are nurtured and developed in much the same way as individuals do.

> **A well-managed team will outperform individual decision makers by 66 percent.**

An empathy-first approach to leading a world-class team starts with developing and communicating a big-picture vision. Teams thrive when they have a clarity of purpose and a common goal. Fostering a shared sense of purpose is key to developing an empathetic bond with your team and will open the door for honest and productive conversations about the team's contributions to your organization. Consider what success will look like a year in the future: perhaps a successful product launch, an exceeded sales goal, or the development of a new and exciting offering. Whatever the purpose, establishing that clarity and defining the road map to success will give the team a clear path to achieving the organization's vision.

Once an organizational goal is established, include the team in the process of establishing its culture. Lead them, especially if it is a more junior team, to established best practices but give each team member the opportunity to shape and define the team's path to success. Not only will team members develop unique solutions when given the opportunity to contribute, but including them in the discussion will also engender loyalty and further cement the deeper empathetic connection between you and your team.

Fostering a culture of open discussion, collaboration, transparency, hard work, and accountability is critical to deepening that connection. Many team leaders fail to make the connection between these cornerstones of good team leadership and the impact on productivity and collaboration. If you've given the team a shared purpose and included them in the process of developing the team's culture, you're off to a good start. Effective empathetic teams need to resolve conflict harmoniously, and there must be a constant reinforcement of the team values. Problems will arise, no matter how dynamic and efficient the team is; they always do. It is common for groups to have conflict when up against a deadline or in the middle of a stressful situation. Infighting and interpersonal conflicts born from different approaches can turn into grudges and lead to disharmony. Disallowing destructive behaviors and addressing conflicts openly with a goal of resolution and harmony will empower teams to solve their problems before they become insurmountable.

Let's look at an example of how one leader can make a change within an organization.

Giving the Team a Voice

Jason entered an organization with a 35 percent turnover rate and was tasked with fixing the problem. Most of the employees worked off-site from the main office and had little interaction with corporate personnel. No one had a good idea of why people were leaving, and every department had their own opinion: recruiters were doing a poor job of identifying talent; managers were disengaged from their employees; the physical distance made it difficult to build relationships; executives did not communicate to the employees; and so on.

Jason developed an employee survey that covered topics such as the organization's culture, compensation and benefits, communication, manager interaction, and executive leadership. The survey was detailed and included multiple-choice questions to determine trends within the responses as well as write-in sections that would allow employees to vent specific frustrations.

The results of the survey were dismal. More than 80 percent of the employees felt disconnected from the leadership team, felt that their voices were not being heard, and wondered about the direction of the organization and their impact on the bigger picture. They also had many varied complaints about the benefits and perks given to the corporate team.

The Lesson: In this example, Jason gave a voice to his team members and collected the results. By making it anonymous, he created an environment where his employees could bring situations to his attention without fear of reprisal. This is an important first step in fostering an environment that thrives on open communication.

While working to define the team's culture, a leader also needs to spend time inspiring loyalty and trust. Team members need to believe the leader will get them across the finish line and that their coworkers will work with them in service to the team's objectives. In the preceding example, if Jason does nothing with the information, employees will begin to lose faith in his leadership.

To build trust, communicate honestly and frequently, and do not hesitate to provide constructive feedback. Be patient; new teams and teams amid change may not operate at their best. Ensure that good performance is rewarded, encourage contribution, and lead by example. The team leader role is to uplift the team and to clear obstacles to success.

Finally, consider team-building activities on a quarterly or semi-yearly basis. Activities outside the office, especially ones that involve a shared goal or objective, can help establish and reinforce bonds. These activities can also be good indicators of who is ready for additional leadership responsibilities. Observe the team when faced with a challenge, as sometimes a leader will step forward to guide the team to a solution.

DEVELOPING THE EMPATHY OF YOUR TEAM MEMBERS

Not everyone approaches situations in the workplace with empathy. Even people with high emotional intelligence can fall short of empathetic reasoning when dealing with particularly difficult situations. Here are five exercises that can help increase a team's empathy.

Exercise: Engaged Listening

If your team is experiencing issues with communication, help them develop their empathy for one another by employing an engaged listening exercise. Even the most frustrating communication problems can become a valuable opportunity to help your team understand the need to participate in conversations instead of thinking about what they are going to say next.

Pair off members of the team and have one person start by telling a story. Then have them switch. Afterward, ask each member of the pair to retell the other person's story, and see how much they retained. Restart and have the first person tell another story. This time, the second person should be encouraged to ask questions, restate situations, and engage with the story. Notice that they retain more information when they are active participants.

Exercise: Debate

Successful conflict resolution is an important trait for an empathetic team. When team members can see other points of view besides their own, they are more likely to come to a resolution without a disagreement escalating. If your team is experiencing issues with conflict resolution, engaging in a formal debate can sometimes help people talk through disagreements while maintaining a level head. Separate into teams that must defend a particularly unreasonable point of view. Perhaps there is a ridiculous customer complaint that everyone is aware of, or unreasonable demands from a contractor. Ask the team to argue the point. Encourage the group defending this point of view to play devil's advocate. This will benefit anyone having trouble seeing things from another person's perspective.

Exercise: Emotional Self-Evaluation

If the team has difficulties with interpersonal communication that stem from frustration or a breakdown in communication, an empathetic leadership approach eschews harsh repercussions, favoring instead regular encouragement for everyone on the team to examine their own emotional state. At regular intervals throughout the day, remind your team to check in with themselves. Suggest that they might like to take a moment to sit quietly for a few seconds and reflect throughout the day as needed. Remind them to ask themselves questions about their emotional state: How am I feeling? Why am I feeling that way?

This may be difficult for members of the team who are not in touch with their own emotional state and do not possess the tools to drill down and understand the root cause of their anger and frustration. The point here is to facilitate a dialogue around why someone may be feeling negatively and encourage a frank discussion among team members.

Putting It Together

Jason brought his managers and team leads into a conference room to discuss the results of the survey. He started the meeting by assuring everyone that nobody was in trouble and that the point of the meeting was to have a constructive and realistic conversation about how to improve things on the team. The mood was tense, so he started by encouraging everyone to take a moment and quietly reflect on the challenges they had been having and imagining what their jobs would look like if those challenges were removed.

He employed active listening to understand the challenges that the managers within his team were having, some of which were directly impacting the challenges that the employees had brought up. He started to see which problems were due to bad processes or lack of tools. He also realized areas where his team had gaps in knowledge that were contributing to the issues.

The Lesson: Jason realized that the problems were fixable, and that with hard work he could get his team members back on solid ground.

DEFINING SUCCESS

The quality of a team's performance depends entirely on its members' understanding of the definition of success. For example, if a team is developing a new software application, success might mean meeting development milestones. Explicitly define the metrics of success to ensure the team shares a common definition. Update your team often about where they stand with respect to these metrics to keep them on track.

Empathetic leadership requires give and take. To ensure a team's continued buy-in, get input from them on what they think is working and where there could be improvement. Request input on their interpersonal dynamics—and even your own performance. Share these results with the team, both the successes and areas for improvement. Celebrate the victories and figure out as a team how to improve.

RETENTION

Increasingly, people are leaving their jobs for reasons beyond salary and benefits. We've seen a shift in the job market as younger generations are focused on more emotion-driven criteria for making a job change. People are more focused on how employees are treated, how the company gives back to the community, and how diverse and equitable the company policies are. Acknowledging these concerns and employing an empathetic approach to retention strategies can have an indelible impact on your organization's ability to keep talent.

In a study conducted in 2018 of 250,000 employees across multiple disciplines, 71.6 percent of attrition was preventable. The following areas were deemed the highest contributors to attrition:

- Career development

- Work-life balance

- Manager behavior

- Compensation and benefits

- Well-being

- Job characteristics

- Work environments

Each of these categories can be improved by building empathy into the retention strategy. Start by soliciting feedback from the individuals in the organization. Use this as an opportunity to get direct feedback on how the organization is doing. Focus on the areas listed here and ask them to rate your organization in each of those seven categories and see where the common problem areas lie.

Perhaps individuals are pleased with their compensation and benefits but struggle to advance their career; perhaps they have excellent work-life balance but no connection to their manager. If the organization is large, the most efficient way to get this feedback is through a survey. An anonymous survey provides the most honest answers. A survey also allows you to aggregate the data and quickly identify trends and weaknesses in the organization. Once the data is compiled, it is imperative to act on it. Giving personnel a voice is only an effective strategy to reduce attrition if they see changes being made.

Some of the issues might be unavoidable due to the nature of your business, or they may be cost prohibitive. All of us would like to make twice our salary and pay nothing for our benefits, but most businesses cannot sustain that kind of cost. Come up with creative, low-cost solutions to help the organization and implement those that will have the greatest immediate impact and are rated most essential by the team. For example,

- Buy an online subscription training program to provide career development.

- Develop a mentorship program that pairs junior talent with senior staff members.

- Create an education and certification incentive program to tie education to monetary rewards.

- Develop in-house training tools and computer-based trainings (CBTs) to train employees on organization-specific information.

My Door Is Always Open

Jason offered himself up to the employees in his organization for one-on-one discussions of their individual frustrations with a promise to take each issue back to leadership with a plan of action. Since many of the employees worked off-site, he took the time to go to them directly and be available in the morning and evening for phone calls. Offering employees an opportunity to vent allowed for them to start to feel like their voices were being heard. Employees were frustrated, but open to the possibility of change.

Based on the feedback provided by his employees, Jason created a list of solutions that could improve team cohesion, morale, and productivity.

Jason identified three key areas that stood out as trends across his teams: manager relationships, corporate communication, and career development. He implemented a career development program and appointed an existing staff member with high emotional intelligence as a specialist to work directly with employees on their advancement. He also introduced new communication strategies for his managers and the corporate officers, and directly addressed individuals' issues where possible.

When Jason could not fix a problem due to a cost constraint, he was honest with the employee and explained why it did not make good business sense.

It took time to right the ship, but within a year the attrition had dropped into the single digits and employee engagement was at a peak. Employee referrals saw a 35 percent increase, the number of employees who received recognition from clients tripled, and the organization's growth spiked tremendously.

The Lesson: In this scenario, Jason reached out and solicited feedback. His engagement and open-minded approach allowed for constructive conversations to happen and to get actionable feedback. As a result, he was able to implement changes that drastically impacted the bottom line.

Keep the lines of communication open, not just between managers and their teams but also with senior leadership. Encourage everyone to reach out directly, make suggestions, and take an active part in the shaping of the future of the organization. Consider offering an opportunity for personnel to provide anonymous suggestions to encourage anyone who feels hesitant in bringing issues to the attention of leadership. Look to the people who are on the ground doing the work every day to tell you what could be improved. Opportunities for betterment can come from anywhere, and sometimes great ideas come from unexpected sources.

Wrap-up

....

The challenges of creating and managing a high-performance team can be met effectively and successfully when approached with empathy. A highly empathetic approach to team leadership will ensure strong performance. The key aspects of developing a high-performance team are—

- Selection of team members to ensure diversity of thought and experience

- Clarity of purpose and goals

- Regular communication of goals, milestones, and expectations

- A culture of openness, trust, and transparency

- Team activities and training to develop empathy

- Focus on retention through empathetic leadership

Chapter 3

Empathy Is the Key to Diversity and Inclusion

The more diversity in an organization, the more overall empathy the organization typically has. Why is that? Because the more individuals get to know and work with people that are different from themselves, the more they can understand their point of view and why they think the way they do. The challenge in the workplace is that people do not often realize there is a lack of diversity. Open discussion and training on empathy can expand an organization's diversity of thought, and help individuals address their biases.

From an HR perspective, diversity policies include things such as avoiding discrimination, employing a diverse set of people from minority groups, and making sure there is no bullying. Is this really all we want for diversity in the workplace?

DIVERSITY OF THOUGHT

A healthy, innovative, creative team needs people with diverse ways of thinking. This diversity of thought can guard against stagnant and rigid ways of acting.

Some leaders, organizations, and companies interpret diversity of thought to mean that a team can be composed largely of the same kind of people with respect to race, gender, age, sexual orientation, socioeconomic background, and so on, as long as they have diverse viewpoints and thoughts. While this might be true to a very limited extent, there is much more benefit to be had by seeking individuals with diverse backgrounds, experiences, and perspectives, which will organically foster a much broader diversity of thought.

Diversity of thought leads to innovation and great ideas, but the price of changing the status quo is the potential for conflict. To weather these growing pains, an organization must undergo a culture shift from hierarchical, top-down decision making to a more flexible leadership model that recognizes challenges from within as opportunities for growth. This requires leadership to embrace the empathetic practices of respectful conversation, active listening, humility, and a bottom-up exchange of ideas.

> Diversity of thought requires leadership to embrace respectful conversations, active listening, humility, and a bottom-up exchange of ideas.

In *The Challenge Culture: Why the Most Successful Organizations Run on Pushback* by Nigel Travis, chairman of Dunkin' Brands, the author discusses why the most effective leaders have people around them with a diversity of thoughts, opinions, and approaches. Travis believes the best way for organizations to succeed in today's environment is to embrace challenge and encourage pushback. He maintains that everyone at an organization must be able to question the status quo, to talk in a civil way about difficult issues, and to debate strategies and tactics without fear of reprisal.

Travis set up what he called "coffee chats," which were made up of people from across disciplines in the organization. The attendees were able to ask him any questions within the bounds of civility. As he said, "The purpose of the coffee chat is to provide an open and safe forum for people to ask questions, share information, articulate ideas, express opinions, and surface disagreements."[1] Arguably more important, Travis also used these meetings to open his thought aperture.

In addition to benefiting the overall health of an organization, there is some evidence suggesting that diversity can also benefit the mental health of an organization's leadership. In business as elsewhere, leaders must resist the insularity that often comes coupled with increased responsibility. The more power someone holds at an organization, the more the people around them will want to please them, in the hopes of earning their favor. This insularity has the effect of narrowing the ideas, thoughts, and approaches that leadership has available at any given time.

Even without consciously seeking it out, leaders can easily find themselves in an echo chamber that's not only bad for business but can also cause much more lasting damage. Jerry Useem, a business author, explored the medical research being done on the brains of powerful people and synthesized his research in an article for *The Atlantic*. Useem theorized that power causes brain damage. Powerful people's mental capacity for reading other people was diminished over time. They lost the capacity for the neural process known as mirroring, which essentially enables people to understand and feel the emotions of others.[2] As described earlier, mirroring is the cornerstone of empathy.

A similar concept is "hubris syndrome," identified by David Owen, a neurologist and former British foreign secretary, and Jonathan Davidson, a professor of psychiatry and behavioral sciences at Duke University. Hubris syndrome is a "disorder of the possession of power, particularly power which has been associated with overwhelming success, held for a period of years."[3] Some of the symptoms of the hubris syndrome are narcissism, contempt for the advice or others, use of power for self-glorification, obsessive focus on personal image, excessive self-confidence, and reckless and impulsive actions.

A culture of challenge, listening to others, and diversity of thought are factors that not only strengthen a business, they also strengthen leadership.

BIASES

The term *bias*, in the context of the workplace, means a person is closed-minded, unreasonable, or unfair against an idea or person. Everyone has biases and they can be unconscious (implicit) or conscious. Biases influence people's decisions and are one of the hardest elements of human behavior to overcome.

"In our brains, there's a stress hormone called cortisol," explains Frieda Edgette, a certified executive coach and organizational strategist. "If you see somebody similar to you, there's little to no effect. But if you see someone different than you, [cortisol] triggers implicit bias."[4] Implicit bias is an unconscious attitude toward a person that influences behavior. This is deep, unconscious behavior that requires work to overcome.

Everyone's capacity for empathy can be weakened by these unconscious attitudes, triggered on a day-to-day basis by our own implicit biases. Most people impede diversity because of limited experiences. Environment, culture, and family all play a part in defining our biases. Insufficient exposure to a diversity of people and cultures is the primary reason for a lack of empathy.

> **We feel stress when we see someone different than ourselves, triggering bias against the person. This is deep, unconscious behavior that requires work to overcome.**

Let's look at the famous case study of Heidi versus Howard. Heidi Roizen was a successful Silicon Valley venture capitalist who became the subject of a case study at Columbia Business School. Professor Frank Flynn presented half his class with a case study with Heidi's name on it and gave the other half of the class the same case study with the name changed to "Howard." The students rated Howard and Heidi equally competent, but they liked Howard and rated Heidi as unlikable and selfish. The students had biases around their expectations for how men and women should act.

Harvard University launched a research project to demonstrate how common hidden biases are. The researchers found that 70 percent (possibly even higher) of hidden biases are directed toward Black Americans, the elderly, the disabled, and overweight individuals. It's also interesting to note that individuals in these underrepresented groups harbor the same level of "bias" as others.[5]

So, is it possible to recognize your own biases and those of others around you? Yes, absolutely. Start by examining your own thoughts and beliefs.

CHECK YOUR BIASES

Be honest with yourself! The only way to uncover your biases is for you to be completely honest with yourself and start examining each individual bias. The first step in clearing out your biases is for you to acknowledge them. Think about how you would answer each of the following questions.

1. What type of neighborhood do you live in or would you like to live in? What are the people like in that neighborhood?

2. Who is your ideal romantic partner?

3. Who would you prefer your children to date?

4. In a crowd, who do you gravitate to?

5. On a dark, empty street, what type of people make you feel nervous or scared?

6. Do you think certain types of people are lazy or without self-control?

7. When you see a name you cannot pronounce, what is your first thought about that person?

Now Reflect: Did any of your answers give insight into your biases? Do you have unease with people who are not like you? Keep analyzing your reactions in everyday life to expose your biases.

BIASES SHOW UP AS FEAR AND ANGER

Humans tend to feel uncomfortable and have anxiety around people who are not like them. This anxiety can present itself as anger and fear.

Anger is the emotional energy you generate to fight against a threat. This occurs even if a threat is imagined. Fear also causes anger as a protection mechanism.

> Anger is a form of self-defense to fight against a threat, even if the threat is imagined.

Think back to the last few times you felt angry or afraid. What were the circumstances? If you dig deep into the situation and look at the root cause, you will find your emotional reaction was solely caused by you. If you can identify what is causing your fear or anger, you can understand and control your reactions to situations and avoid the unintended consequences of bias.

Remember, anger and fear often do not manifest in the ways we expect. Each of the following scenarios is a real-life example of how fear and anger can reveal the hidden biases that drive them:

1. Skipping over a woman's resume because her name was too difficult to pronounce

2. Assuming the man was the senior person in the room and addressing him instead of the woman, who was actually the boss

3. Calling the police when a Black couple were seen in the neighborhood, despite them recently moving into a house close by

4. Rejecting a woman of color for a job because she did not fit in with the corporate culture of golf and beers after work

5. Firing the only Black man in the organization because his manager thought he was lazy, when in reality the task he was given was difficult and no one had trained him

6. Rejecting an overweight person for a job because they did not fit the organization's visual brand

ELIMINATING UNCONSCIOUS BIAS IN THE WORKPLACE

1. **Train your team on unconscious bias and how to recognize their own biases.** The most important step in eliminating biases is to make them visible. Training to put a spotlight on how biases affect decisions and behaviors is critical for people to understand their own biases.

2. **Determine which biases are most likely to affect the organization.** Biases tend to affect functions like hiring and promotions. Understanding where bias is most likely to show up is important when considering important decisions, for example, if a manager consistently gives women a higher performance review than men, or if a hiring manager shuns candidates without "white"-sounding names.

3. **Bring diversity into the hiring process.** Ensuring the organization has diversity is important for making biases visible. Update the hiring process to ensure biases are not involved in hiring decisions. Some of the steps to take are creating a job description that appeals to a diverse pool of candidates; "blind" decision making (remove the name and gender from the resume); and standardizing the interview and decision process.

4. **Encourage a discussion about biases.** Encourage team members to speak up about biases. The more transparent, visible, and open the decision-making process is, the less the organization will be affected by unconscious bias.

5. **Hold managers accountable and set diversity and inclusion goals.** Managers need to be held accountable for their decisions. Use data to analyze managers' decisions on things like who was promoted and the diversity of the hiring.

Changing behavior in the workplace is difficult and may necessitate hard management decisions, like letting go of intolerant and toxic employees. A framework must be put in place that defines the behavior expectations in the workplace, and personnel needs to be measured against this framework.

EMBRACING DIVERSITY

Can people be trained to embrace diversity? Absolutely. There are several ways people can learn to accept diversity. The first starts with really getting to know people. Ask questions about their experiences, what their lives are like, and how their views of the world were shaped. You will be very surprised at what you learn. Actively listen when you ask questions and focus on the other person. Meaningful conversations will give you deeper insight into another person's situation. Leaders should also encourage their teams to learn about each other. To help facilitate this, a leader can publicly recognize accomplishments of people across the organization, show by example by listening to others' experiences, and provide a nonjudgmental space for everyone's input during meetings.

Let's look at a simple example of how asking questions about someone can help mitigate implicit biases.

The Cleaner

Jasmin worked late many nights and usually took time to ask the Hispanic cleaner, Mateo, how his day was. One evening when Jasmin routinely asked Mateo how his day was going so far, Mateo grinned ear to ear and told Jasmin his son had just passed his medical exam and now was a medical doctor. Jasmin was startled, congratulated him, and started asking Mateo other questions about his family: How many children did he have? Where did they live? What country did he emigrate from? Mateo told Jasmin he had owned his own company in Guatemala, but the violence and bad economy made it difficult to survive there. Jasmin found out he had a daughter with a law degree, and another son with a PhD in math.

Jasmin was jolted by this news, because she hadn't realized her own bias. Despite the fact that she acknowledged Mateo every night, deep down she'd assumed he was beneath her—that he was not smart, not disciplined, and that his children would be the same. Instead, Mateo was clearly strong, smart, and disciplined. He'd raised accomplished children despite the significant obstacles he had faced.

The Lesson: Jasmin realized that all the untrue assumptions she had made were due to her bias toward Mateo because he was Hispanic. Her outlook about who he was as a person changed completely once she asked him questions about himself, and actively listened to him.

Another excellent, empathetic approach to reducing the effect of implicit bias is looking for the commonalities between you and another person. Humans tend to focus on the differences between themselves and others. Instead, focus on what you both like. These can be things like hobbies, sports teams, food, clothes, or family. The key to inclusion is finding and connecting through those commonalities. Help your team to connect through common interests. There are lots of ways to help teams learn about one another. The following are three easy techniques that can be relied upon both virtually and in person:

- **Two truths:** Before the meeting, each person sends two statements or truths about themselves to a designated person. During the meeting, the designated person reads each individual's two statements and the team tries to guess who it is.

- **First job/worst job:** In the beginning of a meeting, encourage people to share stories and memories about their first or worst job.

- **Tell me something good:** In the beginning of a meeting, have people share something good that happened to them this week.

INCREASE DIVERSITY WITHIN AN ORGANIZATION

1. **Hire with diversity in mind.** Within an organization, a multifaceted set of changes can be implemented to create a culture of diversity. Carefully examine hiring practices to ensure

they do not reflect hidden biases. Some tips to avoid bias in job postings include using gender-neutral titles; replacing gender pronouns with "you"; and avoiding superlatives such as "expert" and "world-class," which tend to turn off female candidates—who studies show often undervalue their own work experience.[6] During the resume review and interview process, anonymize resumes by removing names and gender pronouns, and develop a predetermined skill priority ranking to avoid ambiguity in the selection of a candidate.

2. **Look at the reward and benefit programs.** Does your organization's culture reward and promote people who bring in new ideas and challenge the status quo? Does the benefit program focus on what is important to different groups of people (e.g., women, parents, older employees, people who practice minority religious traditions)?

3. **Create a culture that rewards listening and incorporating new ideas.** Does the organization regularly have sessions where people across different parts of the organization get together and discuss organizational and process improvements?

4. **Create a feedback culture.** Develop ways for leaders to receive honest, perhaps even anonymous, feedback, and ways to use that feedback to improve the organization.

5. **Switch to an outcome-based organization.** Focus on results instead of processes and procedures. There are usually many ways a task can be done to get to a good outcome. We have

all seen or been a part of an organization where rigid, obsolete processes were damaging morale and efficiency, but leadership upheld the processes because they were familiar, or tied up with the leader's ego somehow.

Wrap-up

....

The more diversity in an organization, the more empathy the organization typically has overall. The challenge in the workplace is that people often do not realize there is a diversity issue. The more individuals get to know and work with people that are different from themselves, the more they can understand other people's point of view. Creating a culture of diversity and inclusion can also increase the organization's innovation and creativity. To create this culture—

- Increase the amount of diversity of thought in the organization by hiring diverse personnel.

- Embrace respectful conversations, active listening, humility, and the exchange of ideas.

- Recognize your own biases (hidden and not) so you can guard against these biases affecting your decisions and judgments.

- Implement training to learn to embrace diversity.

PART II

MANAGING AND LEADING WITH EMPATHY

"Empathy is recognizing a person's point of view
as well as understanding what they feel and why."

L eaders are more effective when they know and understand themselves. Recognizing and understanding emotions in yourself and others allows you to manage your reactions and behavior. This awareness also allows a leader to capitalize on their individual strengths as well as the strengths of their team. Developing empathetic communication techniques is critical to good leadership. A good leader communicates effectively to all different types of people in a variety of styles and mediums. Poor communication can compromise your reputation and effectiveness.

One of the most important leadership skills is being able to confront people constructively and empathetically. The primary issue in confrontation is misuse of confrontation: It is either completely avoided; attempted indirectly; or performed in a harsh, negative manner.

Empathetic communication techniques are imperative when leading through times of change and transition. Managing change, deciding when it's appropriate to begin a transition, and creating and implementing a transition plan are essential skills for an empathetic leader.

Chapter 4

Management Styles and Empathy

A leader's attitude and approach determine the outlook of everyone on their team. Whether a manager is upbeat or negative, determined or resigned, accepting or skeptical, energetic or lethargic, optimistic or pessimistic—whatever their mindset and attitude, it is contagious. The manager sets the tone for everyone else. If the manager is inclusive and listens to other points of view, the team will adopt a style of inclusion and listening. If the manager has empathy, sees the big picture, and has recognized and reduced the impact of their biases, the team will most likely do the same.

The four leadership styles that follow have been partially adapted from studies in the 1930s by Kurt Lewin, who proposed the first framework on leadership styles.

THE FOUR BASIC MANAGEMENT STYLES

There are four basic management styles: Autocratic, Democratic, Laissez-faire, and Nurturing. While these terms may bring up negative or positive connotations, each style has strengths, ways to mismanage, and ways to be empathetic. In addition, a good leader may alternate between these management types depending on the situation, team, or individual they are leading. Great leaders incorporate empathy into their daily management no matter which style of management is required.

The following are basic definitions of the four styles:

- **Autocratic manager:** Retains the power and authority for all decisions, and the team is expected to obey orders

- **Democratic manager:** Encourages all stakeholders to participate in the decision-making process

- **Laissez-faire manager:** Provides little or no direction and gives employees as much freedom as possible

- **Nurturing manager:** Cares for, nurtures, and proactively takes responsibility for supporting others

Let's look at each style in detail.

1. The Autocratic Manager

In the autocratic management style, the manager retains the power and all decision-making authority. An autocratic manager does not typically consult or receive input from anyone else. Instead, the team is expected to obey orders given without explanation. Autocratic managers motivate through a structured set of rewards and punishments.

Historically—especially in military and political contexts—autocratic leadership has dominated management philosophy, but it has also been criticized over the past thirty years as being overly harsh. Autocrats rely on threats and punishment and are usually not perceived as trusting their employees or subordinates. However, this style can be effective when decision-making time is limited and quick, organized action is essential. Unsurprisingly, military leadership is almost always executed in an autocratic style.

This style can also be effective for executing rapid change. For example, if a manager has recently assumed leadership of a poorly managed team in danger of collapse, autocratic decisions may be necessary to get everyone back on track. It should also be noted that autocratic authority is derived from organizational or hierarchical authority; subordinates cannot exercise autocratic leadership of their superiors in an organization.

An autocratic leadership style may be necessary when team members do not understand tasks, procedures, or priorities. In such cases, a manager must make decisions without input from the team until they have been trained and have gotten up to speed.

Autocratic Mismanagement

An autocratic manager makes decisions unilaterally, which over time may cause employees to sit back and wait for direction or, conversely, to become frustrated with the lack of trust and flexibility.

Mismanagement takes many forms, such as: unwillingness to listen to employees, diminishing employees, inappropriate behavior, lack of respect toward employees, withholding information, micromanaging, and creating an environment of mistrust.

Autocratic management is the most likely type of management style to cross the line into bullying, harassment, and violence. These behaviors are unacceptable in any work environment. Inappropriate behavior can take many forms:

- Harassment: offensive, threatening, or sexualized behavior that is unsolicited and may be repeated

- Bullying: repeated abusive and offensive behavior, which in some circumstances may involve inappropriate physical contact

- Aggression: verbal, emotional, or physical violence used to create a fear-based organization

Managing with Empathy as an Autocratic Manager

The autocratic style of management is the one most challenged by the need for empathy. When decisions need to be made quickly and those decisions need to be implemented without question (e.g., in combat), the manager does not have time to listen to their employees' concerns or point of view.

However, many who have served in combat love and respect their leaders because they felt cared for. An autocratic leader must watch over their employees' mental and emotional well-being. Employees will perform much better if their leader connects with them, cares for them, and understands them.

Techniques for Empathetic Autocratic Management

The autocratic leader must positively recognize members, show appreciation, and thank people for their value. The leader may be autocratic in times of crisis or uncertainty, or due to untrained subordinates, but they should still recognize the good work and innovation of team members, even if it's just a thank-you in the hallway as the crisis is going on. People work harder and will go the extra mile if they believe they are part of a team all pulling together for a mission. In sports, a team of superstars can be beaten by a group of lower-skilled people who work better as a team.

Autocratic Amy

Amy was brought in as the new chief financial officer (CFO) of an organization in need of rapid change. The team she inherited was inexperienced, lacking knowledge of any of the processes and financial models required to run the business effectively. Amy wrote new processes herself, and she insisted on reviewing every invoice, payment, and financial report before it was sent out. She kept tight control over the team's every activity. Amy had all of her team take accounting courses so they understood the concepts behind what they were doing. Within a year, the team was producing high-quality output.

continued

Three years later, the team had become more experienced and was chafing under the tight control Amy continued to leverage. More than half decided to leave the organization because of Amy's controlling personality.

The Lesson: In this scenario, an autocratic management style was the correct one to get an inexperienced team on track and learning the skills needed for the position. However, Amy failed to adjust once her team had become more experienced. The autocratic leader must be able to demonstrate empathy by understanding and anticipating the emotions felt by their team members, continuously evaluating the skills and experience of the team, and adjusting their responsibilities accordingly. As the individuals on Amy's team gained experience, she should have started trusting them and delegated responsibility and authority.

2. The Democratic Manager

The democratic leadership style encourages all stakeholders to participate in the decision-making process. The democratic manager keeps their team members and stakeholders informed about everything that affects work, sharing decision-making and problem-solving responsibilities. The democratic leader readily delegates authority to subordinate staff.

This style works best with highly skilled or experienced employees, when implementing operational changes, or when resolving group problems. Democratic leadership provides opportunities for employees to develop a high sense of personal growth and job satisfaction. It is a highly effective leadership style that results in high employee morale, trust, honesty, employee engagement, and productivity.

A democratic leadership style is also effective when a large or complex problem requires input from many people to solve. It creates buy-in from all stakeholders, thus fostering a sense of community and shared purpose.

Democratic Mismanagement

A democratic manager may slow down the decision process too much because of their need for consensus. Mismanagement takes on many forms, such as lack of decision making, wanting to please everyone and thereby being indecisive, and making decisions based on the needs of the most vocal employee.

Managing with Empathy as a Democratic Manager

The democratic style of management focuses on collaboration. Leaders using this style actively seek input from their team members and can effectively communicate back to the team information about why decisions were made. This is a great technique to use when buy-in is needed for a change, idea, or vision.

Techniques for Empathetic Democratic Management

The democratic leadership style lends itself to empathy. The democratic leader needs to listen to all employees' points of view and involve employees to support the problem solving and decision making.

The democratic manager should also employ a coaching technique to help more junior personnel to see the bigger picture and become engaged in the decision-making process.

Democratic Decisions

Mike was the owner of a hardware store and was well liked by his employees. He always asked for input from the employees, really listened to their answers, and considered all their opinions before making a decision. He cared about his employees and they, in turn, cared about him. The store was doing well and had a very loyal, hard-working staff.

Mike thought it might be time to expand the store. He gathered the team together several times to get their input on the expansion. The team gave Mike thoughtful answers about how he could expand. He pondered the decision, continuously pulling employees aside to ask them their opinions. Every day, Mike leaned toward making a different decision based on the last person he talked to that day. The team started getting fatigued with Mike continuously asking their opinions without making a choice. Mike's leadership team started avoiding him because they were so frustrated about his inability to move forward.

The Lesson: Mike's democratic management style worked well for him while the business was in a steady state, but when he had to make a change, his style became dysfunctional. An empathetic leader would have picked up on his team's flagging patience sooner and made a decision so the team could move forward. Additionally, an empathetic strategy would have Mike explain his ultimate decision to his employees and ask for their support during the transition period.

3. The Laissez-Faire Manager

The laissez-faire leadership style is one in which the manager provides little or no direction and gives employees as much freedom as possible. Employees must determine their own goals, make decisions, and resolve problems on their own. The laissez-faire manager is not completely hands-off—they need to be engaged and provide feedback and recommendations to employees for improvement.

This style is effective when team members are highly skilled, experienced, and experts in their field; they are willing and able to make independent decisions for the success of the organization; the roles and responsibilities are clear; they know their roles; and there is little change in expectations, time frames, or constraints.

Laissez-Faire Mismanagement

A laissez-faire manager may evade the duties of management, resulting in uncoordinated delegation. The staff becomes unfocused, without a sense of direction, and dissatisfied. Mismanagement takes on many forms, such as: unwillingness to listen to employees, favoritism, lack of decision making, and inability to get employees engaged.

Managing with Empathy as a Laissez-Faire Manager

A laissez-faire manager typically tells employees where they are going (i.e., the vision) but not how to get there (i.e., the process). The team must find their own way to meet the common goal. To prevent the team from losing their way, even the most laissez-faire manager must recognize that an empathetic approach to leadership sometimes demands that they lead.

Techniques for Empathetic Laissez-Faire Management

Already skilled at letting their team handle the small things, the laissez-faire manager should focus on vision, expertise, and enthusiasm. Their team must see energy and excitement around the common mission, and it is the responsibility of the laissez-faire manager to put extra effort into getting buy-in of that vision. The laissez-faire manager must also pay keen attention to their employees, providing encouragement and making sure people feel valued as members of the team.

Hands-off Leadership

Paul was sitting in his office, typing on his computer, when Melissa appeared outside his office door. She had been working on Paul's team for less than a month. While she liked the fact that Paul gave the team autonomy, she had been floundering a bit trying to figure out what to do with a certain client and was hoping Paul would give her some guidance.

After thirty seconds or so, Paul glanced up and waved Melissa into his office. She quickly explained the issue to Paul, who told her he was confident she could figure this out on her own before dismissing her by going back to his computer.

Melissa gave a sigh, stood up, and walked away, feeling incredibly frustrated. If she could figure it out herself, she wouldn't have come to Paul in the first place. Melissa felt like she was going to fail at her job.

The Lesson: Paul's laissez-faire style worked well with the experienced personnel but was difficult for the younger team members. Paul should have set up his experienced team members as mentors to the younger team members, so they had more direction. Paul should also ensure that his team knows what his vision is, so they have a framework for making their decisions.

4. The Nurturing Manager

In the nurturing leadership style, the manager cares for, nurtures, and proactively takes responsibility to support others. The relationship between the manager and employees is like a large extended family. This style is based on personal loyalty.

Nurturing leadership at its best encourages open and honest

communication, broad-based delegation, and mutual trust, support, and respect for employees and coworkers. It concerns itself with fostering the organization's sense of community. The nurturing manager cares about each individual and expresses interest in their personal life, which gives employees a sense of belonging and being cared for.

This style typically has high employee loyalty, low employee attrition, and employees who feel that decisions are made with their best interests in mind. As a result, this style is best used in organizations where it is critical to keep employees happy and bonded with the manager.

Nurturing Mismanagement

A nurturing manager can mismanage by requiring unconditional trust and loyalty from the employees. If the manager is perceived to favor some people over others, jealousy and anger can cause discontentment within the team, leading to factions and mutiny.

The nurturing manager may not want to make the tough decisions so as not to alienate people or risk creating disharmony within the "family." Mismanagement can take on many forms: lack of decision making, conflict avoidance, favoritism, and decisions based only on employee well-being (and not necessarily what is best for the organization as a whole).

Managing with Empathy as a Nurturing Manager

The nurturing style of management is focused on the individual team members. Leaders using this style actively respect team members and create a sense of community. This is a great management style to use to have a team feel needed and wanted. It is inherently an empathetic management approach. Nurturing doesn't mean indulging or overprotecting, but making sure emotional needs are satisfied so goals can be met. Care needs to be taken not to smother more independent employees.

Techniques for Empathetic Nurturing Management

The nurturing leader is typically empathetic and encourages communication, broad-based delegation, and trust. Team members believe they are cared for.

A Nurturing Nature

Suzie was a very well-liked manager, and her team had the lowest attrition in the whole organization. She spent a lot of time caring for her employees, making sure they were okay, that they had what they needed to do their jobs, and generally being their champion.

One of Suzie's employees who worked at a customer site asked for a raise because his wife was about to have a baby. Suzie believed he had done a great job and deserved a raise. She told him she would give him one and went back to do the paperwork. Unfortunately, Suzie never even thought of checking to see how much the client was paying for his time, and his new salary made the organization lose money on every hour he worked. In addition, there were other employees with the same skills who were being paid less, and there was now an imbalance in salaries across the organization.

The Lesson: Suzie's nurturing style was fabulous for the employees. She truly did care about her team, and they responded positively to her. However, Suzie put the employees' needs above the organization's. Suzie needed to balance both the organization's and her employees' needs.

STRESS-CREATED MISMANAGEMENT

Every manager is under stress at some time. Typically, stress leads to less empathy. People under stress start protecting themselves at the expense of others. This leads to all sorts of mismanagement behavior. Stress can cause a long list of ineffective behavior: a lack of focus, mistakes, anger, bullying, indecisiveness, inconsistent decision making, and withdrawing.

Whatever the form of the mismanagement, the result is a waste of the most important resource in business: the people. Mismanagement can cause discontent, low morale, increased risk of burnout, depression, low sense of worth. The stress to the workforce from mismanagement wastes time and individual productivity; and it loses money for the organization or project.

THE RIGHT APPROACH FOR THE SITUATION

No single management style is better or worse than any other. However, some tasks and positions fit certain management styles better than others. Depending on the situation, each of the four management styles can be appropriate or be destructive. A good leader feels comfortable working in all four styles and applies the correct style to the situation and people. In any one day, it is possible to use autocratic, democratic, laissez-faire, and nurturing styles with different teams or situations.

Practicing using styles that are not as comfortable will increase your range of management skills and will make you a more effective manager. High-functioning managers and leaders can adjust to different situations and use the right approach for each scenario. Let's look at different situations and what type of management is the most appropriate.

1. A manager has taken over a troubled program. The program is behind schedule; the team is in chaos and previously had an indecisive manager. **Autocratic:** This team needs immediate detailed direction and rapid decisions to get them back on track.

2. There is a team of very senior engineers who are employed across the whole organization as subject-matter experts. **Laissez-faire:** The team does not need day-to-day direction; they are self-sufficient and make their own decisions on their day-to-day activities.

3. A reorganization just occurred with a new set of effective and strong managers. **Democratic:** Use the experience of the team and engage them in all the decisions.

4. A team of engineers ranges from junior to senior in experience. The engineers work at customer sites and are dispersed across a large geographical area. **Nurturing:** Since the engineers all have different work locations and take their day-to-day direction

from the customers, what they need from their manager is to know someone cares about them.

5. There is a part-time sales team whose members' ages range from 18 to 22 years old. None of the employees have more than six months' experience. **Autocratic and Nurturing:** The team needs step-by-step instructions and detailed management because of their lack of experience. In addition, they need to be mentored and feel they are cared about.

6. A new team started with a mix of people across the organization. Some are good engineers, and some were put on the project because no one knows what else to do with them. **Democratic and Autocratic:** Use the experience of the good engineers and create a democratic environment where they are included in the team's decisions. Evaluate the other personnel to determine their experience level with the work being done on the project. Provide the less experienced personnel with more detailed tasking, and make decisions without their input.

7. An existing project has been going on for ten years. The teams are established, the work is well defined, and, in general, the whole team is running well. **Democratic and Laissez-faire:** The team members are experienced and work well together. Use their experience and include them in decisions. Make sure they are a part of the direction and vision of the project. The team needs very little day-to-day management, is self-motivated, and can work independently.

EMPATHY IN MANAGEMENT

So how does empathy play into each of these management styles? Empathy is recognizing another person's point of view. Empathy helps us see the big picture and removes ego and judgments when communicating. Managers can become more empathetic by increasing their listening skills. Active listening is not only hearing the words the other person is saying but also understanding the full message. Try not to be distracted, and refrain from formulating an answer or thinking of other things while the other person is still talking.

Steps of Active Listening

- **Pay attention:** Look at the speaker; put aside distracting thoughts.

- **Show you are listening:** Nod occasionally; smile and use facial expressions; have an open posture.

- **Provide feedback:** Use terms like "what I am hearing . . ." or "what do you mean when you say . . ."

- **Defer judgment:** Allow the speaker to finish and don't interrupt with counterarguments.

- **Respond appropriately:** Be open and honest; treat the other person in a way you would like to be treated.

The Unhappy Employee

Arthur set up a meeting with one of his employees, Tom. In recent days, Tom had been vocal about his dislike of a change Arthur was making to reduce the number of people on the help desk team. Tom showed up for the meeting with Arthur on time, but Arthur was late getting back to his office. As a result, Tom sat waiting for ten minutes by himself. Once Arthur came in and sat down, he proceeded to tell Tom that he needed to stop bad-mouthing his decisions. Put on the defensive, Tom started explaining why he felt the way he did, but Arthur received a ping on his phone, immediately picked it up, and started texting back.

Noticing that Arthur was on his phone, Tom stopped talking. When Arthur was finished, Tom began explaining again, but halfway through Tom's first sentence, Arthur cut him off. Arthur said that he made the decision to save money, that it was final, and that Tom needed to get on board. Then he stood up and opened his door, dismissing Tom.

Constructive Solutions

Arthur arrived a few minutes late to the meeting, offering an apology to Tom for holding him up. Arthur turned his phone on silent and sat down. Arthur said he'd heard that Tom was unhappy with the decision to reduce the help desk personnel, and then invited Tom to share his thoughts about the matter directly. Tom explained that the reduction of help desk personnel put more pressure on the software development team, making them less productive and putting them in danger of missing their deadlines for an upcoming software release.

Arthur paid attention to Tom while he was speaking. Once Tom had finished, Arthur summarized the issue, saying, "Having fewer help desk personnel means the software development team is fielding more trouble tickets, giving them less time to write software." Tom nodded emphatically. They were on the same page.

Arthur then explained to Tom that the project was over budget and needed to reduce costs across the organization. Arthur thought that reducing a few help desk personnel was the least painful way to reduce cost. He then asked Tom earnestly if he felt there was another way to reduce costs on the project. Tom thought for a few minutes and told Arthur he now understood the reasoning behind the decision.

As for reducing costs, Tom said there was a senior engineer whose role on the project was over. In addition, there was also a customer who would pay for this senior engineer to support the design of a new financial system. If they moved this senior engineer to another contract, they could then keep three of the help desk personnel in their roles. Arthur nodded and said he thought that would work. He stood up and shook Tom's hand and went on to implement the new plan. In the next staff meeting, Arthur gave Tom credit for the innovative idea to save the jobs of the help desk personnel.

Wrap-up

No management style is better or worse than the others. Each style can be effective and positive, and each management style can be misused. The four styles need to be applied to the appropriate situation, or low morale, discontent, and low productivity can result.

- The **autocratic** style: Effective when decision-making time is limited; quick, organized action is essential; executing rapid change is required; or team members do not understand tasks, procedures, or priorities.

- The **democratic** style: Effective when the team is highly skilled or experienced; implementing operational changes; resolving group problems; or complex problems require input from many people to be solved.

- The **nurturing** style: Effective when it is critical to keep employees happy, loyal, and with low attrition. This style provides a sense of community and belonging.

- The **laissez-faire** style: Effective when team members are highly skilled and experienced and are willing and able to make decisions for the success of the organization; the roles and responsibilities are clear; everyone knows their role; and little change is expected in expectations, time frames, or constraints.

Chapter 5

Empathetic Leadership Starts with You

"Is 'tough empathy' an oxymoron? In business, empathy is often seen as soft, but research makes it clear that exceptional leaders are highly empathic *as well as* hard-headed."[1]

—Joshua Freedman, CEO of Six Seconds,
the global emotional intelligence community

What makes you want to follow or work for one person and not another? Whom do you remember as the best leader you ever followed? What was the nature of that person's character? What made them so special?

Chances are, that person made you feel authentically cared for. Some of the greatest leaders of our time were not only tough and demanding but also fair and empathetic. Throughout history, leaders of all walks of life have found success in applying the principles of empathy to garner love and loyalty without compromising their overall vision.

Dr. Martin Luther King, Jr. was an example of a leader who embodied tough-mindedness, determination, persistence, and empathy. Dr. King made it a point to spend time listening and understanding the people he was fighting for. He also did not give in when he encountered confrontation. He was tough but empathetic.

Microsoft CEO **Satya Nadella** shifted the focus at Microsoft to start with empathy. Under Nadella's leadership, Microsoft has been extremely successful, taking the market capitalization past $1 trillion. In his book, *Hit Refresh*, Nadella states, "At the core, *Hit Refresh* is about us humans and the unique quality we call empathy, which will become ever more valuable in a world where the torrent of technology will disrupt the status quo like never before." Nadella also stated, "Empathy makes you a better innovator [because it helps unlock] unarticulated needs of customers."[2]

Nelson Mandela, a South African anti-apartheid revolutionary who served as the country's president from 1994 to 1999, led through empathy and not authority. His political opponents had far more authority, power, and money. In fact, they put him in prison for life. He chose empathy for a regime that took away his freedom and his family, that tortured and assassinated his close friends. Nelson Mandela used empathy to build bridges and disarm his political enemies. Mandela was released from prison after twenty-seven years and became the first Black president of South Africa. In Mandela's own words, "You don't address their brains, you address their hearts."

Apple CEO **Tim Cook** has increased the organization's value by more than $1 trillion since he became CEO. For years, Cook has urged empathy. In Cook's 2017 MIT commencement address, he told the graduates: "People will try to convince you that you should keep empathy out of your career. Don't accept this false premise."

Five Things Empathetic Leaders Do

1. Know themselves

2. Work on increasing empathy

3. Empower their teams

4. Align people in positions to maximize each individual's strengths

5. Consistently motivate and inspire

Let's take a closer look at each of these attributes, especially as they apply to strong, empathetic leadership.

KNOWING YOURSELF

Learn Your Hidden Biases, Strengths, and Weaknesses

Leaders are more effective if they make decisions without undue influence from their personal biases, ego, and judgments about people or situations. Individual egos and biases produce blind spots and cloud judgment. The more you know yourself and have worked on your biases, the easier it is to make objective and fair decisions.

Anger and Fear

Anger is the emotional energy generated to fight against a perceived threat. Anger manifests as a result of fear.

Let's look at some of the things that leaders commonly fear, which can cause them to become angry with their subordinates:

- Lack of respect

- Loss of status

- Negative judgment

- Letting go of what is known or comfortable

- Failure (i.e., others' poor performance will reflect negatively on their own)

When you feel angry, step back and take the time to think about the reasons for your anger. Ask yourself these questions:

- When do I feel angry?

- What fear is the root cause of my anger?

- How did my actions contribute to my anger?

- Why do certain people trigger strong reactions in me?

- Do I dismiss individuals' opinions without really taking them into consideration?

Pay attention to how you react throughout your day and begin learning about yourself from the patterns you're able to discover.

Growth as a Leader

To remain effective, leaders must continue to grow. Every situation you encounter presents you with a growth opportunity. This includes occasions when something does not work out the way you planned. Everyone fails from time to time. The distinguishing feature of great leaders is that following failure, they know how to get up, keep going, and learn from their mistakes.

Individuals notice when their managers grow, change, adjust their opinions, and admit shortcomings without becoming paralyzed by fear or self-doubt. One of the most important skills to learn is how to accept criticism. Listening to what others have perceived to be harmful, and to understand how to grow and change, is a difficult but necessary step to becoming a great leader. It requires stepping back, not letting emotions cloud the response, and seeing the issue from another's point of view. Accepting and internalizing criticism can be difficult and unsettling at first but it also leads to extremely powerful personal growth. And of course, it also serves as a powerful example for your team.

Three Steps to Level Up Your Personal Growth

1. Request and receive regular feedback from a trusted mentor.

2. Conduct a "personal lessons learned" introspection every week that includes these questions:
   a. What went well?
   b. What could I have done better?
   c. When did my fear or biases cause me to not listen or to handle a situation badly?

3. Meet monthly with coworkers and colleagues and perform a group evaluation of the past thirty days. To get honest answers, people need to feel like they can trust you. That might mean you need to open up first about something you could have done better, let the team talk about it, and allow them to see you accepting criticism.

BOOSTING EMPATHY

Empathy can be learned and improved by practice, but it means working on being self-aware, recognizing different perspectives, and listening to understand.

Being Self-Aware

When encountering a situation that causes you to have an emotional reaction, ask yourself why you reacted to the situation in that manner.

Reflect upon those actions after the fact and dig deep. Shift the focus from *what* you are feeling to *why* you are feeling it.

Once you have started to identify why you are reacting to certain situations, work on channeling those emotional responses into something constructive. It is not possible to stop having emotions, but it is possible to learn to control how much they run your life, and what you do with them.

Recognizing Different Perspectives

Once you feel you have started to understand yourself and your emotions, then pay attention to the verbal and physical reactions of the people you are talking to. Ask them how they are feeling. Engage with them genuinely and look for ways you can improve their situation. Insight into others' emotional states allows for better understanding of their actions.

Of course, it is impossible to fully understand another person and their experiences, so the best approach is to understand their perspective by recognizing the emotions they are having.

Listening to Understand

Finally, go into every situation with an open mind. Listen to your team, your coworkers, and your peers. Leave your ego behind and engage with the people around you. This allows for better understanding; for better ideas and solutions to be considered; and for a stronger, more trusting team.

> Don't confuse empathy with making
> people happy or being nice.
> Empathy enables you to understand the people
> around you, to make better decisions, to
> communicate clearer, and to inspire loyalty.

EMPOWERING YOUR TEAM

Allow the Team to Make Decisions

One of the worst things that can happen to a high-performance team (or any team, for that matter) is for all the decisions to be made by their manager. Organizations that foster this kind of micromanagement typically grind to a halt when the leader is busy or out of the office. Over time, teams become disgruntled, and personnel with innovative ideas and self-motivation leave the organization.

There is a significant difference, however, between micromanaging and leveraging control. Leveraging control means telling the team *what* they need to do. Micromanagement is telling them how to do it. The difference between the two is huge. There is a time and place for micromanagement, but it should only happen for specific reasons and for short bursts of time. For example, micromanagement can be good when a team or individual needs to learn new tasks or skills or when an employee is struggling and needs more guidance and oversight.

An empathetic leader sees the value each employee brings to the organization and can delegate and empower people to bring out their strengths. How can you create an environment allowing for and accommodating the appropriate sharing of decision-making responsibility? First, your team must operate in an atmosphere of trust.

Create an Environment of Trust

Trust encourages teams to work together to solve problems. When a team has a culture of trust, both from management toward the team and vice versa, there will be more disclosure of information, more acceptance of others' ideas, and a more comfortable, relaxed, and creative atmosphere. In an environment of trust, ideas are encouraged and fostered. Work becomes exciting because people feel like they are part of the solution. Trust is an amazing team-building tool.

So, how do you create a trusting environment? The first way is to have integrity, do what you say you will, and always follow through with action. The second way is to share information so people are not forced to make assumptions. In both cases, it is critical to be honest in all communication. The only way to create a trusting environment is to communicate frequently, openly, and honestly.

MAXIMIZING INDIVIDUAL STRENGTHS

Know Your Team and Their Talents

It is imperative for a good leader to analyze team members to find out their natural talents and skills. Take the time to learn who is good at what: Who always nails deadlines? Who excels at innovation? Who is great with customers?

Then, realign the staff to take advantage of their different skills. Aligning people based on their talents requires flexibility, initiative, and energy. The alternative, however, is a team that doesn't feel seen as individuals, and as a result does not trust its leadership. No one wants to feel like a cog in the machine, and the experience of being a misused resource does nothing to inspire loyalty among employees.

> **Empathy allows a leader to learn about their team and align people based on their different strengths.**

Define Clear Authority and Accountability

How do you feel when you do not know who has the authority to make a decision? When no one is accountable, what happens to the goals?

An empathetic leader defines clear roles, responsibilities, and authorities for everyone under their charge, because they know that one of the worst situations an employee can face is to be given responsibility for a task without the authority to get it accomplished. For example—

- Being assigned a task without being given the resources and people with the expertise required to do the work
- Being a program manager with responsibility for managing

the cost, schedule, and tasking, but who must get approval from the boss for all decisions

- Being assigned to manage a team without the authority to reprimand or promote any of its personnel

- Being given an unreasonable deadline without any input over the scope or dates

MOTIVATING AND INSPIRING

Show Passion and Excitement

A passionate leader will promote excitement throughout the team. Who would you rather work for? A manager who is excited and happy about coming to work each day, or a manager who is indifferent and distracted?

A team with inferior resources and equipment who possesses great passion and commitment will almost always outperform a team with a ho-hum attitude, even with the benefit of state-of-the-art resources. As a leader, it's up to you to exhibit a sense of excitement and anticipation about what you are doing. This attitude is contagious—and that's a good thing.

Be a Role Model for Ethical Behavior

Leadership sets the culture and tone for both the organization and its teams. If the manager sets a high ethical standard, the culture becomes one of similarly high standards.

But why is it important to have an organization with high ethical standards? What does it mean to be involved in an ethical organization or team? How do you set and maintain a high ethical standard? And what does this have to do with empathy?

Ethics is the process of determining right and wrong. Organizations with high ethical standards are characterized by honesty, clarity, and openness. Risks of all types are reduced, because collaboration and honest discussion typify the team, from top to bottom. This environment yields high-trust relationships among employees and between teams and their managers—because when employees feel seen and trusted, they are more likely to see and trust in turn.

Therefore, it benefits the empathetic manager to show their team, by words and actions, what is right or wrong for the organization's culture. If a team sees their leadership lying to clients or cutting corners, they will assume that type of behavior is acceptable. If team members see their manager take home office supplies or waste work time with personal activities, they will assume these behaviors are acceptable for them as well. This can cost any organization valuable time and money.

High ethical standards reduce organizational risk.

Of course, it is easiest to behave ethically when things are going well. Even people who believe they are ethical will sometimes behave unethically when an organization, team, or project gets in trouble. The most common example of this is lying about the status of a task. Employees lie because they fear reprisal or do not have a sense that their superiors will be understanding. A team that hides or lies about status is in big trouble—not to mention ineffective.

To resolve this,

- Keep communication open without reprisals for making mistakes or delivering bad news.

- Keep listening to your team and determine a course of action together.

- Actively manage risks to promote honesty and clarity.

Positive Energy Creates More Positive Energy

Both positive and negative energy from a leader permeate throughout the organization. A wave of positive energy can pull people together, makes them believe in their mission, increases productivity, and saves money and time. Negative energy from a leader, on the other hand, only creates more negative energy. The team may spend time complaining, whining, and not focusing on success. Such teams typically end up over budget and past deadlines.

Things will go wrong. Staying positive doesn't mean ignoring anything bad that happens. In fact, pretending everything is okay when it is not can be extremely detrimental and frustrating to a team. Instead, projecting positivity means recognizing and acknowledging the bad things, but then looking at what can be done to solve the issue rather than wallowing in negativity.

Care about Your Team

Have you ever had a boss you believed really cared about you? How did it make you feel? Didn't you work harder for that person?

Demonstrating authentic caring does not mean a leader isn't tough or demanding—just that they truly care. And from your own experiences, you can see how that authenticity tends to inspire loyalty and investment. So now how can you, as a leader, show you care?

Listen. Leverage an empathetic strategy by listening more and talking less. Do not assume that everyone wants to listen to you talk. There may be extraordinary ideas, opinions, and thoughts you miss out on just by failing to listen.

Recognize. Give employees a thank-you in front of their coworkers or give them a small token or gift card to provide recognition of their hard work.

Remember. Ask about individuals' personal lives and remember what they say in order to follow up again later. Acknowledging their birthdays may seem insignificant but can go a long way toward making someone feel cared for.

Be real. Provide kind but honest feedback to employees. This might lead to some uncomfortable conversations, but it also means you care enough to tell the difficult truth.

Be transparent. People can tell when they are not receiving the whole picture. Trust the team and help them to understand the bigger picture.

Wrap-up

....

Successful empathetic leaders do these five things:

1. Know themselves and their biases, strengths and weaknesses

2. Work on increasing empathy

3. Empower their team by delegating responsibility and author-
    ity to make decisions and provide an environment of trust

4. Understand each individual's talents and help maximize
    their strengths

5. Motivate and inspire the team by having excitement, passion,
    and ethical behavior

Chapter 6

Developing Empathetic Communication Techniques

How do you communicate in your organization? Do you know how much contact the people around you prefer or need? Do your team members need to hear from you frequently to feel comfortable that everything is going as planned? Does your customer prefer email, phone calls, or face-to-face meetings? Do your coworkers like you to pop by for quick conversations or do they prefer email and texts?

The more a leader knows how their team likes to communicate, the better the rapport—and the more efficient the organization, tasks, or team become. An effective manager collaborates and builds relationships at all levels of the workplace community.

Why else does good communication matter?

1. Effective and authentic workplace communication improves productivity and morale.

2. Absenteeism and turnover rates decrease when good communication is valued within an organization.

3. Employees feel valued and secure when they receive frequent and truthful communication from their supervisors.

4. Teams with strong communication work more efficiently.

5. When people know their own role and responsibilities—and their value within the organization—they are more productive.

6. Productive employees with high morale means happier customers, which can translate into business growth.

Good communication skills help build good relationships. Part of being an empathetic manager is recognizing what communication techniques work for different teams and people. Different personality types may respond better to different techniques for the most effective communication.

Poor communication can compromise a manager's reputation and effectiveness. Any person (e.g., team member, customer, member of another department, someone in the broader community) can either derail or enhance an activity, team, or task. To leverage the whole community, it is critical to build relationships with all stakeholders.

To be a successful empathetic leader means you must be able to communicate effectively with all different types of people in a variety of styles and mediums. The basic types of communication are face-to-face, video, telephone, email, and texting.

Let's talk first about nonverbal communication including body language, gestures, paralanguage interaction (i.e., voice, volume inflection, and pitch), facial expressions, and appearance. Albert Mehrabian, a respected expert on human communications, did some groundbreaking research determining that communication between humans is approximately 55 percent body language, 38 percent tone of voice, and 7 percent what you say. In other words, 93 percent of communication is nonverbal.[1]

Think about it: An estimated 93 percent of human communication is nonverbal and paralanguage. These cues provide valuable information, determining in many cases how a message is received. Furthermore, another person's nonverbal, paralanguage, and body-language feedback can help us understand what the person is actually feeling and allow adjustment on what is being said and how it is said.

> **An estimated 93 percent of human communication is nonverbal and paralanguage.**

Nonverbal clues provide context for understanding another person's emotions and thoughts. When someone's words and body language are not consistent, people will believe the body language every time. Body language betrays what we are really thinking and feeling. People can sense when there is a mismatch.

What She's Not Saying

With great trepidation, José knocked on his boss's door for their scheduled meeting. From behind the door, Alycia told him to come in. She was sitting at her desk and asked José politely to sit down. Alycia had arranged herself in her office chair so that she was sitting slightly sideways. It seemed to José that she was looking just above his head. He started to get a bad feeling. Alycia told José that he was an important member of the team and she needed him to complete his project without being distracted.

Despite her calm words, Alycia's legs were jiggling and she crossed her arms over her chest as she told José that he may hear rumors of a layoff, but his job was safe. José nodded and rose to leave. He felt very uneasy, not sure why he did not believe her.

The Lesson: Alycia's efforts to reassure José fell flat because her body language and her words did not match. That night when he went home, he updated his resume and started to search for a new job.

Decoding someone's body language can be difficult. In José's situation, Alycia's body language showed that she was lying. She would not face him but sat sideways. She did not look him in the eye and then when she was telling him his job was safe, she crossed her arms.

While the behaviors José picked up on are common tells, trust your gut instinct.

According to *Inc.* magazine, here are five signs someone is lying to you.[2]

- **They touch their face, mouth, or throat.** This touching occurs because of the fight-or-flight response and stress.

- **They repeat themselves.** The person is buying time to think about what to say next.

- **They pause before answering.** This is especially true if the answer is simple or obvious, because they are trying to keep track of what has already been said.

- **They look toward the door.** This is part of the flight response: we look toward where we want to go.

- **They don't blink.** Practiced liars want to telegraph confidence so they look at you without blinking.

Remember, these five signs are just guidelines. Sometimes people exhibit the behaviors listed if they are very stressed, but not necessarily lying.

What is or is not acceptable body language also varies from culture to culture, and what is polite in one culture may be offensive in another. For example, in the United States, eye contact is considered a sign of confidence, but in some countries unbroken eye contact is considered aggressive and confrontational. Sitting cross-legged is seen as disrespectful in Japan, and showing the soles of your feet is rude in some Middle Eastern countries. If directly communicating with people from another culture, learning their norms will help to avoid unintended miscommunications.

ACTIVE LISTENING

Active listening, described in Chapter 4, is a vital component of empathetic communication. Active listening builds trust and strong relationships, alleviates conflict, and helps understanding.

Often when people talk to each other, they do not listen attentively and do not engage enough to feel empathy for the person they are listening to. They are distracted, half listening, or busy formulating a response to what is being said. People assume they have heard what the other person is saying, so instead of paying attention, they focus on how they can respond to prove their point.

Active listening has several benefits. First, it forces everyone to listen attentively to others to be able to accurately reflect what has been said. Second, it avoids misunderstandings because listeners confirm they do really understand what another person has said. Third, it tends to open people up and to get them to say more. In active listening, the listener does not have to agree with the speaker but still works hard to understand. If more clarification is needed, the listener can repeat back what was said. This has the added benefit of reinforcing to the speaker that they are being listened to intently. If the listener has not properly understood, the speaker can further explain. Active listening is especially useful during confrontation.

COMMUNICATION TYPES

There are four basic communication types: individual face-to-face (including video); group meetings; telephone (audio only); and email and text. In different situations, each type of communication has its strengths and weaknesses.

Face-to-Face and Video Communication

Face-to-face meetings are the most effective type of communication technique for building empathy, collaboration, rapport, and confrontation. In any situation involving face-to-face communication, it is important to stay engaged in the current conversation. So many times, cell phones and other interruptions are distracting and have the effect of making the other person feel unimportant.

It is worthwhile to note that the COVID-19 pandemic caused a substantial rise in remote work, causing a shift in communication techniques for many companies. Face-to-face meetings of all kinds have been reduced or discontinued altogether in many workplaces. Reducing face-to-face meetings may be safest and most efficient, but face-to-face still remains the most effective type of communication for building empathy.

Video meetings are a great alternative if face-to-face is not possible. Much of the paralanguage (voice tone, inflection, volume, pitch) and nonverbal information such as facial expressions are available, which can help build empathy and collaboration. With video meetings, do not be tempted to check email or look at a phone off-screen.

Everyone can tell when someone is not paying attention when their eyes are not straight on the camera.

Regardless of whether your face-to-face meeting is in-person or remote, in some cases it may be appropriate or necessary to accept a call, or answer a text or email, but please apologize and explain why the interruption is necessary. In fact, if you anticipate an urgent or important call, it is a good idea to say that at the start of a conversation.

In this next scenario, let's look at how interruptions damaged a new employee's impressions of an organization.

Paula and Ed: Bad First Impressions

Paula came to HR to pick up the new employee, Ed. Paula welcomed Ed and started walking down the hall to introduce him to the team. Her phone buzzed and she rapidly starting texting. Ed had to wait awkwardly while Paula finished her text conversation.

Then, Paula brought Ed to meet the marketing director, Ashley. Ashley got up from her desk and shook Ed's hand, welcoming him on board and giving him a brief description of her role. Paula interrupted Ashley with feedback on an ongoing project, launching into all her comments as Ed stood by, wondering what to do.

Finally, Ben came by and told Paula he needed to talk to her immediately. Paula left the office and walked out with Ben, leaving Ed standing there.

The Lesson: Feeling unvalued by his boss as a new employee, Ed wondered why he had taken this job and considered putting his resume back up on job sites.

Paula and Ed: Getting It Right

Paula came to HR to pick up the new employee, Ed. Paula welcomed Ed and started walking down the hall to introduce him to the team. Her phone buzzed and she quickly put it on mute as she continued down the hall.

Paula then brought Ed to meet the marketing director, Ashley. Ashley got up from her desk and shook Ed's hand, welcoming him on board and giving Ed a brief description of her role. Ben came by Ashley's office and told Paula he needed to talk to her immediately. Paula said she would come to his office after she finished introducing Ed around to the team. Ashley smiled and told Ed to have a good day. Paula then finished introducing Ed to the rest of the team.

The Lesson: Ed felt welcomed, valued, and respected because the leadership team took time out of their day to welcome him and introduce him to the rest of the team.

Group Meetings

Meetings have an important place in most offices and enterprises, as they streamline group communication and information sharing. Group meetings may occur in a face-to-face setting, or via video and teleconferencing. No matter the form, all group meetings can be difficult to run effectively because people bring in their own personal agendas. It is paramount to have a clear goal for any meeting or presentation and to communicate the desired outcome to all attendees at the start.

Group meetings are an effective and necessary tool for managers. Meetings occur for many reasons, including sharing status and necessary information, brainstorming, or managing change. Empathy is the key to a great meeting. Meetings are a chance to read the dynamics of the team, understand the hidden (and sometimes not hidden) conflicts, adjust expectations, and support team collaboration. In addition to empathy, meetings need to be managed effectively, including the use of an agenda, advance preparation, exercising control over the time spent on each topic, and taking written minutes to ensure all actions and decisions are documented.

Sometimes meetings are not effective because one person dominates and does not allow others to speak. The meeting leader must learn how to manage such disruptive individuals. Some techniques for managing a dominant personality in a group meeting are as follows:

- Gently interrupt the person and state that there is only so much time left to hear everyone's opinion.

- Listen to the dominating person but maintain a neutral expression. Avoid any response because it may encourage them to continue to talk.

- Thank the person talking and redirect the conversation to someone else ("Thank you, Tom, for your thoughts. Mary, what do you think?").

- If you are interrupted, politely insist on finishing ("José, I would like to finish my points if you don't mind" or "Would you mind giving me one more minute to finish my thoughts, please?"). Another technique is to ignore the interrupter and keep talking. They will get the point that you are not conceding the floor to them.

Teleconferencing and videoconferencing now allow remote attendance at many meetings. This poses additional challenges to the person managing the meeting. It is even more important to be clear about the agenda, the expected meeting outcome, and the time allotted for each topic. In teleconferences, if meeting attendees become disinterested, they may put the meeting on mute and check email, hold other conversations, and even walk away from the computer or phone—hardly an efficient way to accomplish the goals of the meeting.

The following is an example of a meeting with both in-person and teleconference attendees where the project manager was not prepared for the meeting.

Adam's Teleconferencing Tragedy

Bob popped his head into Adam's office, calling out, "Hey Adam, everyone is waiting for you in the conference room." Adam looked up, realizing what time it was. He was late for the meeting. Adam grabbed his computer and ran into the conference room. He hurriedly opened up his computer and brought up the presentation. That was when Adam realized he'd invited some remote team members and

continued

he needed to open up the teleconference. Meanwhile, everyone in the conference room was on their phone answering email. Rodney's phone rang and he got up, stepped out, and answered the call. Once the teleconference line was open, Adam hurriedly connected to the conference room projector to present the material. Meanwhile, Melissa had stepped out of the meeting to talk to the receptionist about an event coming up.

Adam had already begun digging into the information on his slides when one of the remote attendees asked if he could send them the presentation so they could follow along. Adam stopped his presentation to send an email with his presentation material. Meanwhile, everyone could hear typing on the teleconference line as the remote attendees did other work. Adam was never able to get the attendees to focus on his presentation and he ended the meeting early.

The Lesson: Adam wasted everyone's time with his lack of preparation. Let's look at the same scenario showing a better way to handle the meeting.

Adam's Drama-Free Presentation

Adam set the alarm on his computer to go off twenty minutes before the start of the meeting. He grabbed his computer and headed into the conference room, wanting to make sure he had everything set up before the meeting's start time.

He opened up his laptop and sent the presentation to everyone on the meeting notice. Then, Adam turned on the projector and connected to it, making sure the display was correct. He then opened up the teleconference bridge and started greeting people as they dialed into the meeting. His presentation was crisp and clear, and there was a great, focused discussion. Adam took notes during the meeting. After the meeting had ended, he typed up the notes and distributed them to the attendees.

The Lesson: Adam respected people's time and ensured everyone in attendance could fully engage by distributing the material in advance. His on-time, crisp meeting made people feel valued and respected.

Telephone Communication

Telephone communication is necessary especially with remote teams or customers, but is more challenging because of the reduced amount of nonverbal information available from the other person. There is no body language or facial expressions to help convey the message, so the words, tone, and inflection alone must do the job. The natural cadence between people when they talk is also disrupted, due to the lack of visual clues as to when the other person is finished speaking.

Let's look at a scenario where a person was unprepared for the phone conversation.

Tom: Hello.

Avery: Is Tom there?

Tom: Speaking.

Avery: Why are the IT guys not here to install all the computers?

Tom: Can you let me know your name and organization?

Avery: I am the new project manager in the software development department, and I was told the IT people would be here this morning.

Tom: Would you please let me know your name and project?

Avery: Avery, and I am in charge of the move of the software team to the new building.

Tom: Can you provide me with all your contact information so I can make sure you receive all of the correspondence related to your project? I'm pulling up the recent communication and the IT team was told to delay the install until next week.

Avery: Ugh.

Tom: Yes, let me get your contact information and I will send you all the information.

Avery did not make it clear who he was and the context around his call. The receiver had to take the lead in the conversation, making Avery look unprepared and unprofessional.

The next scenario describes a more polished and professional way to handle the discussion.

Tom: Tom Diver, IT manager, speaking.

Avery: I am the new project manager for the software development team, Avery Allen. I am taking Jennifer Herror's place. I was told by Jennifer the schedule for the computer installations was starting today. I'm calling because I have not seen any personnel yet to start the installation.

Tom: Hi, Avery, nice to meet you. Welcome aboard. I'm pulling up the recent communication and the IT team was told to delay the install until next week. If you provide me with all your contact information, I can make sure you receive all of the correspondence and the updated schedule related to the project.

Avery: Thank you.

Tom: I would love to set up a time to meet face to face to go through all the details of the project with you. Can you meet this afternoon? Three o'clock? I can come to your office.

Avery: Yes, thank you. Three o'clock this afternoon is perfect. See you then.

The second conversation works because the caller identifies who he is and gets straight to the point. The communication is clear, direct, and does not take up any unnecessary time. Both speakers are professional and helpful, and the conversation ends on a positive note. Telephone etiquette is a part of the general impression you give people.

Email and Texting

These two means of communication are worldwide, nearly instantaneous, and can be used to communicate with a number of people at the same time. They are powerful tools if used with discernment. While great for quick exchanges of information and data, email and texting are very easy to misinterpret, simply because the personal element is almost completely missing. Much of what we feel and think comes out in our paralanguage and nonverbal communication.

Email and texting do not provide nonverbal cues, so it is easy to convey the wrong message, and just as easy to receive and interpret an email or a text incorrectly. While some may attempt to use "emojis" or texting codes such as "lol" ("laughing out loud") to convey emotional context, these shortcuts may not provide the exact emotion you want to convey. For all these reasons, if you need to have communication with someone that involves potentially emotional content or that must function to build rapport, email and texting are almost never the correct choices.

There are, however, instances when these rapid methods of communication can be extremely useful, so let's take a closer look at their principal strengths.

Email

Most managers receive a huge volume of email. To be most effective, emails need to have a clear purpose. If extended dialogue is required (for example, if it is going to take more than two rounds of replies), communication should take place in a phone conversation, video teleconference, or meeting. However, email works well to disseminate information to a large number of people. It is asynchronous (the sender and receiver do not have to communicate at the same time), which works wonderfully for communicating to teams with busy schedules, distributed across time zones (or even on different continents), for information and data sharing, and for communication of noncritical or noncontroversial data.

The following example illustrates an overly detailed, complex email with multiple topics. The recipient did not read all the way through the email, and that led her to misinterpret what she read and to not respond to all the requests. Read for yourself and see if you can follow along:

To: Customer
From: Project Team Lead
Subject: Status

We are still having trouble with the system around the inventory management. We don't think we can get this fixed for two or three days. The API from our accounting system tool to the inventory management is not working and the SQL database is not being updated. We have called the application's tech support and we are having them help us with the problem. We do have a work-around and the team has been trained on it.

I also wanted to know if we could schedule a joint happy hour party with our team and your team. Would you be willing to pay for half of the event?

continued

Finally, Joe came by today and provided me with a list of additional requirements for the project. I will have the team analyze the requirements and give Joe feedback.

The Lesson: The email did not get to the point fast enough, was full of technical jargon, and contained multiple topics in one email. The email failed to show empathy with the customer. It does not take into consideration that the customer was feeling extremely stressed that the system was down. It should have communicated in the subject line or the first sentence that the system is up and running. It is very common for readers to just glance at the first part of an email before responding. In this case, the customer never read the part stating there was a work-around or the other two topics in the email but jumped to the conclusion that the system would be down for two or three days, which led to an extremely angry call to the project team lead.

The next example suggests a much better way to deliver the required information by breaking it up into three separate emails with unique subject lines.

To: Customer

From: Project Team Lead

Subject: Inventory Management System Is Up and Running

The inventory management system is fixed with the exception of two minor functions, for which we have an acceptable work-around.

Please let me know if you would like additional details on the system status.

Thank you so much.

To: Customer

From: Project Team Lead

Subject: Happy Hour / Team Build

Hi, I hope your day is going well. As we previously discussed, I would like to schedule a joint happy hour with our two teams. I have very reasonable quotes from some local restaurants. If we split the cost, it would not be burdensome for either organization.

Thank you so much.

To: Customer

From: Project Team Lead

Subject: New Requirements

Hi, I wanted to let you know that Joe came by today and provided me with a list of additional requirements for the project. In order to make sure my team understands your intent completely, would you mind having your system engineers and my developers meet face to face early next week? We would like to start the development as soon as possible.

Thank you so much.

The Lesson: The last set of three emails are very clear on the question being asked and the response required. They omit unnecessary detail. Each email has a specific topic, so the recipient can read it easily and send back a quick response. Empathetic emails are developed with an understanding of the audience, and their needs and concerns. In addition, emails may need to be forwarded on to different people. For example, the first email may need to be sent to senior customer leadership, the second email sent to the customer finance department, and the third email to the customer system engineering team.

Texting

Texting is a focused, one-on-one electronic communication method. Text messages are typically shorter and quicker than emails, and some shortcuts in typing are acceptable. It is an excellent technique for yes or no answers or quick information sharing.

Since it's also more casual than email, texting is great for communicating with people you already know. However, texting has limitations in a work environment. Text messages cannot be easily forwarded or archived, and formatting is limited.

Here are some good texting rules to follow in the workplace:

1. Limit the use of abbreviations and emoticons.

2. Texting in incomplete sentences is okay but may seem rude to some people.

3. Reread your text before sending, especially if you use the voice-to-text feature, to limit the misspellings.

4. Keep the text short and to the point. However, be aware of your tone. Short texts can sometimes be interpreted as harsh.

5. Sign your text if you do not regularly communicate with a person by text. The person receiving the text may or may not have your phone number in their contact list.

6. Refrain from texting detailed information or data that will need to be referred back to at a later date. Texts are not as easy to track and organize as email.

Wrap-up

Effective, authentic, and truthful communication improves productivity and morale; reduces absenteeism and turnover rates; and increases employees' efficiency, productivity, and feeling of being valued.

Each communication technique has advantages and disadvantages, depending on the situation and persons involved.

- **Face-to-face meetings** are the most effective type of communication technique for building empathy, collaboration, and rapport. Face-to-face meetings are the most effective for confrontation.

- **Video meetings** are great if face-to-face is not possible. Much of the paralanguage (voice tone, inflection, volume, pitch) and nonverbal information is available, so this technique can help build empathy and collaboration.

- **Group meetings** streamline group communication and information sharing. They may occur in a face-to-face setting, or via video and teleconferencing. Group meetings can build rapport and build relationships.

- **Telephone communication** is necessary with remote teams or customers, but is more challenging because of the reduced amount of nonverbal information available from the other person.

- **Email** is worldwide, nearly instantaneous, and can be used to communicate with a number of people at the same time. Email is a powerful tool if used with discernment. While great for quick exchanges of information and data, emails are easy to misinterpret because all the nonverbal communication cues are missing.

- **Texting**, like email, is a powerful tool, especially for exchanges of quick questions, information, and data. However, texts can be easily misunderstood because they are typically very short and devoid of nonverbal cues.

Chapter 7

Effective Confrontation through Empathy

T hink about how you understand the word *confrontation.*
For many people, it brings up all sorts of strong thoughts,
beliefs, and emotions. Do you see confrontation as unpleasant, aggressive, or negative? Does confrontation—the way you
understand it—have a place in an empathetic work culture?

Confrontation does not have to be difficult, and it does not have
to come with unpleasant aftereffects. In fact, occasionally, confrontation is necessary in order to resolve issues. Handling confrontation in a
constructive manner is imperative for a well-functioning team, but it is
often misused—and attempted through indirect, back-channel means,
conducted in a harsh and negative manner, or avoided altogether.

Applying empathy in the context of confrontation requires us to hold in mind what empathy is and what it is not. Empathy is seeing the bigger picture and understanding the impact of a conversation for all parties involved. It is the act of releasing ego, anger, fear, and judgment while communicating with others. Empathy is *not* sympathy or pity. It does not mean that you are dissuaded from having a difficult conversation by someone's emotional state.

Empathetic confrontation creates a common vision going forward by presenting the issues in a way that reduces emotion for both parties. The goal of empathetic confrontation is not to produce separation but rather to create unity. The most effective confrontation is where emotions and ego are put aside and the discussion centers how to solve the issue.

To reach this goal, you must first understand how you react under stress. Leaders need to be honest with themselves! It is important to pay attention and recognize stress and figure out what works to defuse that stress before it harms your team.

> **The goal of empathetic confrontation is not to produce separation but rather to create unity.**

Confronting someone from a place of anger, of course, is one of the worst and least productive ways to work through an issue. Someone who confronts their subordinate in anger may see short-term benefits, but there will always be lasting negative effects. When you are angry, step back and take the time to think through why you are reacting:

What is the basis for your anger? You must diffuse your feelings of anger and stress before your communication can be effective.

These seven practical steps can help foster empathy and productive confrontation.

EMPATHETIC CONFRONTATION: SEVEN STEPS FOR SUCCESS

1. **Determine a common goal for the meeting.** Make sure the meeting is only about this goal. Confrontation is about helping the other person and resolving a specific issue. Keep your mind on resolving the issue—not berating the other person or making them feel bad. The less emotion that is brought to the discussion the better.

2. **Do not make a play for the other person's emotions.** Most people do not care what you feel, think, or believe—especially when they feel uneasy and stressed themselves. Focus the discussion on the issue. Do not bring in your anger, fear, or ego. This is about the other person and not about you. This is not the time to try to get sympathy (e.g., "your performance is making me look bad"); to vent your anger to make yourself feel better; or to be arrogant and state how much better you could do their work.

3. **Make sure you understand your own reactions.** What are you invested in? What are you reacting to? Why are you angry? What are your motivators? Being right? Doing things your

way? Making everyone on the team happy? Remember that
in the vast majority of cases, even when it seems someone is
attacking you, they're usually only protecting themselves from
a perceived threat.

4. **Find a way to help the other person save face.** Saving face
    means preserving "self-esteem, self-worth, identity, reputa-
    tion, status, pride, and dignity."[1] This means to respect the
    individual and be willing to give the other person a way
    to renegotiate their position to preserve their dignity. It is
    detrimental during confrontation to cause shame, fear, and
    anger in others. This breaks down trust and creates a fear-
    based environment.

5. **Tackle the underlying issues and not the behavior.** Figure out
    why they are acting the way they do by asking questions and
    listening to them, to determine the root cause.

6. **Do not presume to know what they think.** Avoid asserting
    that you understand the other person or their position on
    the issue. The reality is that you almost never have the whole
    picture—especially from another person's perspective—only
    what they choose to share with you.

7. **Present constructive options to the individual you are
    confronting.** Creating a respectful way out of confrontation is
    an act of great maturity and enlightened, empathetic leader-
    ship. Be careful, however, to avoid providing choices you do
    not have the ability to follow through on, that you do not
    really agree with, or that you know the other person would
    not agree to.

> **Most of all—
> be kind,
> listen.**

It's important to understand that empathy is not always warm and fluffy. Empathetic confrontation is the result of a leader having balance and a high degree of self-understanding. It is hard to confront someone in a productive manner when you're afraid, angry, or anxious.

Empathetic confrontation focuses the discussion on the facts, rather than venting or satisfying the needs of your personal ego. Remember, empathetic confrontation isn't about you, the initiator. It's about the facts and the situation.

When confronting someone, make the meeting only about that one issue. Do not sneak in other things. If too many things are discussed in one meeting, it does not allow the focus to be on a solution to that one issue. Do one thing at a time.

Following is a scenario where a manager was able to confront an employee and develop a solution that worked for both of them.

Dig Deeper

Don walked by Melissa's cubicle yet again. She was late! He was so irritated—this was the third time this week. Don ran a tight ship, and he expected his employees to be on time every day. He huffed in anger and walked back into his office. Melissa ran in looking very harried, threw her purse on the floor, and got to work. Don knew he needed to confront Melissa.

continued

Don's first impulse was to stride over to Melissa's cubicle and insist that it was unacceptable for her to be late repeatedly. He wanted to tell her not to do it again. Instead, he sat in his office and took a deep breath. Don knew he needed to calm down before talking to her. Melissa was a good employee and worked hard.

Once he had regained control of himself, Don went out and saw Melissa talking to a client on the phone. He asked her kindly to come by his office when she was finished. When Melissa came to his office, she had her head down and there were tears in her eyes. She clearly thought she was going to be fired. Instead, Don gently asked her to sit down and tell him what was going on that was making it hard for her to get to work on time. Melissa whispered that her car broke down and she could not afford to repair it. She was taking the bus to work, and she was still trying to figure out how to get her daughter to day care with enough time to catch the bus and get to work on time.

Don was a little shocked and he wondered why Melissa hadn't told him before. She was a good employee, and her job did not involve working closely with other employees. Don took a leap and asked if she wanted to work from home for the next month until her car was repaired. He warned her that he would be monitoring her work closely and if she was not keeping up with her workload, he would cancel the work-from-home option. They discussed the parameters and rules he required if she worked from home. Melissa smiled, thanked him profusely, and told Don he had nothing to worry about.

The Lesson: Melissa was relieved to have the flexibility to work from home while she saved enough money to get her car repaired. Don felt good because he was able to help keep a strong, loyal employee and adjust her work situation so she could be more productive.

This second scenario shows how a manager was able to confront someone with bad behavior and turn him into a productive employee.

The Gossip

Mary walked down the hall and saw Jerry moving from one office to another. She was furious. Every afternoon without fail, Jerry went from office to office, talking to each person, spreading gossip. He was behind in his work, and for the work he did get done, he always seemed to get help from other people. Mary opened her mouth to yell at Jerry to get back to his own desk before she realized that was unprofessional and unproductive.

Instead, Mary went back to her office to think about why Jerry irritated her so much. Was it because he didn't work hard and he also made others less productive? Was she hurt because she felt he was talking about *her*? Was she upset because he never came by to talk with her and she felt left out?

Mary realized some of her reaction was because Jerry never came by to talk to her and she imagined he was talking about her, though she did not have any evidence. However, the fact was that Jerry was not getting his work done and usually took more than an hour in the afternoon talking and joking with others. She decided to confront him just about how his work was not being completed.

Instead of formally calling Jerry into her office, she casually stopped by his office. Mary asked him how his day was going and calmly listened to him talk about what was going on with him. After they talked

continued

for several minutes, she brought up that he was not completing his work. Jerry admitted he was bored, didn't like the tasks, and he hated sitting in his office by himself all day long. He asked Mary if there was any other work that was more people-oriented, even if it was small. She thought about it and realized she had some customer outreach activities that had been put on the back burner.

He was such a good talker that she thought she should use it for good. Jerry jumped at the chance. It was just what he wanted to do! Mary then let him know that he should only walk around and talk to people for about fifteen minutes in the afternoon before getting back to work. Jerry nodded and agreed.

The Lesson: Mary was able to confront bad behavior in a way that both saved face for the employee and set him up for success in the future.

As you can see, in each case the initiator of the confrontation focused the discussion on the facts rather than venting or satisfying their own needs. This is perhaps the most important aspect of empathetic confrontation: The confronter must have sufficient self-understanding to avoid acting while stressed or out of control. Remember, empathetic confrontation is about communicating effectively to remove the roadblocks to success.

Wrap-up

....

Confrontation does not have to be difficult or nerve-racking. There are seven simple steps to take for productive and meaningful confrontation:

1. Determine a common goal for the meeting.

2. Do not make a play for others' emotions.

3. Make sure to understand your own reactions.

4. Find a way to help the person save face.

5. Tackle the underlying issues and not the behavior.

6. Do not presume to know what they think.

7. Present constructive options.

Chapter 8

Managing Empathetically during Transformation or Change

One of the most difficult times to manage people is during a change or transformation. People resist any change, even if they know it is for good. This resistance triggers fear and defense mechanisms. As a result, building trust is one of the most effective ways to manage change. Trust opens up sharing of information, feelings, and opinions, allowing leaders to understand and build relationships with the people they lead, creating a stronger workplace community.

Let's define change and transformation. Change is modifying day-to-day activities and processes to achieve a desired result. Change is getting a better version of what you have. Transformation is creating something new. A butterfly is a transformation, not a better version of a caterpillar.

Change can be small and incremental or large and complex, but it is not a fundamental adjustment to the framework of a team or organization. Transformation is always larger, more complex, and necessarily disruptive.

Both change and transformation can be disturbing to your team. Care needs to be taken for each one but especially transformation. Let's first look at how to manage change.

MANAGING CHANGE

A leader's responsibility to an organization is to continuously analyze its processes, roles and responsibilities, tools, people, and structure; and to determine the changes required for improvement. Even the most successful and established organizations undergo change in one form or another.

One of the best ways to manage change is to set up a continuous evaluation and process improvement culture. Continuous process improvement with empathy at the core can bring diversity, creativity, and employee engagement into an organization and should be embedded into a team or an organization's standard business rhythm. An empathetic, continuous process improvement culture engages personnel across various functions in the organization. This cross-section of personnel provides a basis to break down communication silos and bring in understanding and trust across the organization.

It should be noted that while change in a large company or

organization must be more formalized than in a smaller one, effective communication and trust is critical no matter how large or small the team.

This trust provides a framework for employees to feel comfortable and take risks by providing their ideas for change. Fostering a culture of continuous process improvement can yield benefits far greater than paperwork-sparing processes and fewer meetings.

Continuous process improvement is the ongoing effort to bring the organization's products, services, culture, or processes to a higher quality or effectiveness. When empathy is brought into the continuous change process, people are more likely to speak out, feel trusted, and find better ways to improve processes.

Some of the benefits of continuous process improvement are—

- **Increased employee morale, retention, engagement, and lower turnover:** If employees recognize their input is valuable and they can have a direct impact on the organization's success, then they will be happier, be more engaged, and feel like they are part of something larger than themselves.

- **Better customer service:** A continuous process improvement culture will not only affect internal processes and employee engagement but will also translate directly to the customer's experience. Employees who are constantly thinking about ways to improve internal processes will also look for better ways to improve the service they provide to their customers.

- **Keeping a competitive edge:** Looking at continuous improvement pushes employees and managers to look beyond the status quo. It requires employees to try something new and look at novel technologies and processes. This, in turn, keeps the organization competitive and on the leading edge.

When setting up a continuous evaluation and process improvement culture, one important step is to set up a process improvement team with a cross-section of people and roles in the organization. This team will be tasked with listening to suggestions, evaluating the suggestions, and championing the subsequent changes—becoming ambassadors throughout the organization.

To set up a process improvement team, there are important questions to answer that need to be communicated throughout the organization, not only to the team itself.

- **Vision:** What are the focus and goals of the process improvement team? Examples of different goals are to save money, to improve productivity, to improve morale, or to improve working conditions.

- **Budget:** What budget threshold does the team have authority to spend before they need to request approval? Some changes require an initial investment but will ultimately save the project or organization money. Require a financial trade-off analysis and a pro/con analysis so the team has the most information to make the decisions.

- **Authority:** What responsibility and authority does the team have that does not require any upward approval? How does the approval process work? An effective process improvement team needs to have the responsibility and authority to make decisions and implement change. It is utterly frustrating for a team to have great ideas and no authority to implement any change.

- **Lead:** The lead of the team needs to be given the guidance to make sure everyone is heard, and no one dominates the conversation.

- **Team:** The team needs to be carefully selected to have a diverse set of people from across the different departments in the organization.

- **Frequency:** The meetings need to be regularly scheduled and treated seriously. They should only be rescheduled for an emergency or another very important meeting. Every two weeks is a good rhythm—holding the meeting too often means the status gets repetitive, but too far apart means there isn't any pressure to complete actions in a timely manner.

- **Suggestion box:** It is important to solicit ideas for process improvement from everyone in the organization, so having some type of anonymous suggestion box allows for everyone's ideas to be brought up to the process improvement team. Decisions around each suggestion need to be sent out to the whole organization.

- **Tracking:** It is imperative to assign each action to an individual with a due date, and to track the status at each meeting.

- **Documentation:** Documentation of each discussion and decision is absolutely necessary. The whole organization needs to
  see success and progress. Listing all the improvements, large
  and small, on a whiteboard or other visible place in the office
  (virtually or physically) gives the whole organization a feeling
  of success.

MANAGING TRANSFORMATION

Sometimes complete transformation must be implemented to take
over new markets, to save a company from failing, to take advantage
of an acquisition of another company, or to react from a technology
innovation or outside forces. Let's look at a few recent transforma-
tions due to COVID-19:[1]

- **Commercial airlines offering cargo shipments.** With drastically fewer commercial passengers, airlines used the empty
  passenger cabins to transport much-needed items, including
  health care provisions.

- **Grocery stores becoming fulfillment centers.** A number of
  grocery stores converted stores to fulfillment centers for rapid
  delivery of orders.

- **Hotels offering day rates for work-from-home employees.**
  With hotels nearly empty, Red Roof hotels started offering
  day rates for remote workers needing fast internet and
  a quiet atmosphere.

- **Restaurants partnering with tech companies to increase mobile ordering capabilities.** For example, Papa John's now offers Facebook instant ordering. These partnerships allow brands to serve customers more quickly and efficiently.

- **Fitness companies moving to online workouts.** With physical locations closed, fitness companies switched to live-streaming exercise classes and released at-home workout plans.

Companies, organizations, and sometimes programs and projects, grow like stair steps—they hit platforms then jump up. The jump-ups can be difficult and may require a transformation instead of incremental change.

The same people, processes, and tools that were great when the organization was small may not work as the organization matures. The same holds true for a project: the same people, processes, and tools that worked during the start-up period may not be effective when a project gets into the steady state or needs to meet certain milestones.

The type of leadership that is effective in a small, cozy business may not be the same leadership that succeeds in a large, international organization. As your team, project, or organization transforms, the leadership needs to transform along with it.

It takes an empathetic and visionary leader to recognize when it is time to transform the organization. Empathy is looking at the big picture and understanding the needs of others, such as clients, employees, and business stakeholders. If a leader stays myopic and insular, they may miss the signs that a transformation is becoming necessary to ensure a strong, thriving business.

Timing of the Transformation

How do you know when it is appropriate to transform your organization rather than continue implementing incremental changes? To see the warning signs clearly, an organization's leader must be able to tap into an empathetic strategy where the needs of their own ego take a backseat to the broader picture of the organization and its future.

Following are some of the signs that it is time to transform a company or organization.

Loss of market share: When market share is declining, it is imperative to transform quickly or the business may not be relevant to customers. There are many examples of large, extremely successful companies that failed to transform when they started to lose market share: Kodak, Xerox, Blockbuster, Yahoo, IBM, JCPenney, Blackberry, Myspace, Sears, Polaroid, RadioShack, and so on.

Business expansion: Business mergers, takeovers, or organic growth are all instances where transformation is necessary or the business will falter.

Employee dissatisfaction or attrition: Dissatisfied employees can negatively affect the team or organization because their motivation to perform is reduced, and they become a disruptive force in the organization. Some reasons why employees are dissatisfied are lack of recognition, lack of trust in the organization, benefits that do not match the industry norm, salaries that are too low, lack of career growth, poor management, and lack of input into the business.

Customer dissatisfaction: Is the product or service offering becoming obsolete? Is the team not providing the expected customer service? Do employees have the expected skills and knowledge the customer requires?

Reduction in productivity from employees: Employees want to be productive and make a difference. Processes that are obsolete and time-consuming, micromanagement, and lack of appropriate tools or infrastructure are some of the big reasons for a reduction in productivity.

New strategy: A new strategy is sometimes developed to preempt a major disruption or change to the business market. When a new strategy is developed, the processes, people, and structure of the existing team or organization will most likely feel disconnected with the new strategy. Supporting the new strategy may also require a change in the leadership and people in the organization.

There are several notable examples of companies that developed a new strategy requiring significant organizational change. Each company listed could have stayed the same but developed a bold strategy that transformed the company.

- In 2013, Netflix's CEO detailed a commitment to move from distributing content to becoming a leader in original content. This announcement caused significant internal transformation resulting in Netflix tripling in size in five years.

- Neste moved from a regional oil and gas company to a global leader in renewable biofuels.

- Western Union started out as a telegram company and is now the largest money-transfer service in the world.

- Nintendo was a playing-card company that transformed into one of the largest online gaming companies in the world.

- Corning started out by developing glass bulbs for Edison, and in the 1970s produced fiber-optic cables capable of transmitting huge amounts of data. Corning invented Gorilla Glass, which is installed in every generation of iPhones.

External economic or market change: COVID-19 is an example of a rapid market change that required many companies to rapidly transform or go out of business. Market change may also be due to changing regulations, technology advances, or supply chain disruptions.

Five Steps to Implementing Change and Transformation

There are five actions a leader can take to help implement a change or transformation with ease.

1. **Create a vision and goals for the organization.** The first step is to have a vision and organizational goals that can be articulated clearly and easily. The vision provides a framework around which to make decisions, which naturally will have a radical effect on the decisions made. Here are a few examples of how different visions affect decisions in an organization.

» If a company's vision is to grow as fast as possible and sell, it would be better to put resources into high-impact teams for short-term growth rather than a long-term investment.

» If the company's vision is to have a long-lasting, multi-generation family business, the focus should be on slow and careful growth for a sustainable, long-term business.

» If the team's goal is to grow market share, marketing would be a high investment, and the team would typically have less overall profit in the short term.

» If the organization has an overarching vision to have happy employees, the investment would be for employee benefits and other strategies for making the organization the best place to work.

» If the program's vision is to please the customer stakeholders, the focus would be on continuous customer interactions that may take the focus away from other activities.

2. **Create a plan that translates the vision into actionable steps.** Create a step-by-step list of activities and a schedule for the transformation. It is critical to have actionable and clear steps in the plan. Bring in stakeholders to review the plan. Put in resources and costs for each activity to make it clear to all stakeholders the transformation costs in time, resources, and opportunity. It is important to be flexible and agile during the transformation process, but the steps will provide a framework for the transformation.

3. **Create a team of people that are champions of the change.** The champions can be stakeholders, members of the staff, or anyone to help with the plan. The process improvement team is a great starting point for creating a team of champions from different parts of the project or organization. Once that team understands the vision and the necessity for the transformation, they can evangelize and communicate the change across the organization.

4. **Develop a communication plan to give frequent and regular updates to the whole team.** It is critically important to over-communicate to anyone affected by the transformation. Provide regular updates and be honest on what is working and what needs to be adjusted. This ensures the team isn't surprised by any negative feedback.

5. **Have a retrospective every week.** Be honest and go through what is working, and what is not working, in the transformation process. Recognize any disgruntled people and make a plan to provide additional communication to them.

Why Do Transformations Fail?

1. **Lack of leadership buy-in to the changes:** Many times, the leaders leading the transformation resist the change. They have not embraced the transformation themselves, even when they know it is necessary.

   » Fear will come up during a transformation, even for the

leadership and champions of the transformation. The fear of the unknown, the fear of failure, the fear of not being good enough, and the fear of not being respected are all part of transformation. The leadership team needs to face these fears and deal with their own emotions thoughtfully and responsibly before they fully embrace the transformation.

2. **Lack of a clear road map and vision for the change:** It is extremely frustrating to be told about a transformation and not have any road map or plan for implementation. It creates chaos in the organization, people start making power plays, productivity is negatively affected, and employees become dissatisfied.

   » A plan needs to be developed before the start of any transformation. The plan should be detailed but also have flexibility to adapt to any unforeseen issues. The plan should identify risks and have contingency plans for each risk. It is important for risks to be identified up front, with ways planned to mitigate the risks and to minimize the real-time fixes to issues in the middle of the transformation.

3. **Lack of flexibility to adjust during the transformation process:** It is very rare for any transformation to work exactly as planned. Leadership will be required to adjust and be flexible during the transformation and to communicate the reason for any adjustment.

   » Transformation plans should have extra scheduling and costs built in for unforeseen issues. Daily status meetings to identify issues and make rapid adjustments are critical to allow the team to adapt activities before minor issues become major risks to the transformation.

4. **Poor communication about the transformation:** Frequent and detailed communication is required for any successful transformation. When people are not given information, they tend to fill in the blanks with negative thoughts. To prevent this, over-communicate to the team.

5. **Resistance to the transformation:** The most difficult time to manage people is during a change or transformation. People may resist any change out of habit, even if they know it is for the greater good. Fears during transformation need to be addressed. Let's look at common fears and how to address them.

Common Fears during Transformation	How to Address Fear
Fear of job loss	Show the team the new organization chart with their names on it. It is imperative to be honest, though. If there will be layoffs during the transition, carry them out quickly to reduce fear in the rest of the team.
Fear of the unknown (fear of failure in the new environment)	Communicate the vision and goals of the changes. Provide mentors from the transition team and/or training to get personnel comfortable in the new environment.
Fear of not fitting into the new structure	Provide to all personnel a reporting structure with clear roles and responsibilities.
Fear of failure or of learning a new skill	Provide training for the new environment and assure personnel that they will have time to learn the new system.
Fear of status loss or redefined identity	Personnel that the organization values for their expertise may be fearful that their status is in jeopardy. Clearly communicate their worth to the organization and provide mentoring and training.

Wrap-up

People resist change and transformation. Fear of the unknown triggers emotional responses in most people. Leadership must take care in implementing a change or transformation. Engaging employees for continuous process improvement is a very effective way to have champions of the change within the organization.

The five steps to take to implement a change or transformation are as follows:

1. Create a vision and goals for the organization.

2. Create a detailed plan (schedule, resources, cost, etc.) with actionable steps to translate the vision into reality.

3. Create a team of champions of the change.

4. Develop a communication plan.

5. Have a retrospective every week to determine if an adjustment is needed.

Watch out for the pitfalls of transformation:

• Lack of leadership buy-in to the change

• Lack of a clear road map and vision for the transformation

• Lack of flexibility and agility during the transformation process

• Poor communication about the transformation

• Resistance to the transformation

....

PART III

GROWING A BUSINESS THROUGH EMPATHETIC LEADERSHIP

Empathy is understanding what someone needs
and figuring out how to give it to them.

Every organization is unique, and each has a set of priorities and challenges requiring a customized approach to achieve success. Understanding what is needed is the first step in attracting a team of individuals to execute the vision. Applying an empathy-based approach to hiring is a proven method to ensure the organization has the right people in the right positions.

Regardless of the product or service, the organization is solving a problem for someone. Engaging with potential customers by creating relatable, targeted content takes an in-depth approach to what people need.

Finally, understanding a customer's fears and challenges provides a unique opportunity to increase engagement and sales. Nobody enjoys receiving a sales call, but most people will listen to a pitch if it clearly solves a problem they are experiencing. Customizing and targeting communication throughout the entire sales process results in higher customer engagement and better relationships.

Chapter 9

Empathy and Hiring

I t is no secret that employees drive a business's success, so when designing a talent acquisition strategy, the primary question should always be, "How do I attract a diverse, engaged, and qualified pool of individuals that want to work for my organization?" Where an empathetic leadership approach has the edge in achieving this goal is in viewing the hiring process as a two-way discussion with a potential employee. Many organizations' hiring practices focus on whether a person fits the organization's needs. Expanding the conversations with candidates to identify their motivations will establish a stronger relationship and better understanding as to how the individual can contribute to the organization. More important, it will build a bond of trust with the candidate as they start to see you as an ally in their journey to find a new job. These days, candidates are interviewing you as much as you are interviewing them.

According to a study by Businessolver,[1] more than two-thirds of surveyed employees in technology, health care, and financial services reported that they would take slightly less pay if an employer has a compassionate, empathetic culture. Let's look at how the organization's vision and needs can be articulated better throughout the hiring process.

> **More than two-thirds of employees would take less pay if an employer has an empathetic culture.**

WHO DO YOU REALLY NEED?

The most integral part of any hiring campaign is fully understanding what the organization needs. Too often, hiring managers will fail to break down a job to its component parts and think through the hard and soft skills it requires. This can result in the position "evolving" throughout the interview process or after the candidate is hired, as the hiring manager further refines the requirements and identifies the true needs of the organization.

The whiplash candidates experience when an organization does not establish what it is looking for before starting interviews can have negative implications not only for the position, but also for the organization's reputation. It also can result in identifying the wrong person for a job, or lead to new employees feeling as though they have been misled.

When a manager within your organization identifies a need, it's important that there are established processes to create the best job description by understanding the position requirements.

Following are examples of best-practice questions to ask internally before candidate interviews begin, to solidify the parameters of the position and anticipate what an employee in that role might need for success. The insight gained in answering these questions should be used to inform the hiring process.

What must the person filling this role possess to be successful? This is not the same as "what skills do they need." Think of it like this: What skills or experience cannot be taught or learned on the job? Does this position require the ability to work independently, think critically, and learn quickly?

What will success look like? Think ahead six months. What would the person in this role need to have accomplished to be successful? This insight can shed light on everything from identifying the right person to structuring a successful onboarding.

What are the team dynamics? Is there a certain type of person who would fit in well with the existing team? Does the team have similar viewpoints that could benefit from a new perspective? For example, do you have a team full of task-oriented, introverted engineers and need someone with a high emotional intelligence to balance them out?

Where and how can this work be performed? This is an opportunity to open the aperture to a more diverse pool of candidates. Can this position be remote? Are there accommodations that can be made so this position can be filled by someone who is differently abled?

Sometimes it's hard to see the forest for the trees; managers can get stuck on one skill requirement or work methodology. It's important to have another department—talent acquisition, human resources, etc.—challenge the hiring manager to dig into the preceding questions and think outside the box. Once the true need for the organization is determined, it's time to begin to craft the specifics of the job and put together guidelines for identifying the talent needed to fill the position.

CREATING AN EMPATHETIC JOB DESCRIPTION

You know who your organization is looking for. Now what? You need a branded job description that captures the attention of talented people. Your organization needs to stand out among its competitors and be the most attractive option for job seekers. The goal here is to get the ideal applicant to visualize themselves in the role and be excited enough about it to apply. It is important to use language that is inclusive to attract a wider range of candidates who can visualize themselves in the role. Job descriptions that are not inclusive may deter a candidate who could be perfect.

An Inclusive Job Description

1. **Avoids overly complicated requirements.** Data suggests that there is a significant differential in the ratio of male and female applicants for jobs with long requirements lists; men are more likely to apply for a position if they meet most of the requirements, whereas women are likely to apply only if they meet 100 percent of the required qualifications.[2]

2. **Eliminates "he" and "she" pronouns, keeping the job description gender neutral.**

3. **Replaces gender-coded words and phrases such as "rock star" and "ninja" with straightforward titles.** While these words may seem harmless and add flavor to a description, the imagery they conjure can alienate exceptional candidates who may not feel comfortable describing themselves in those terms.

4. **Describes the role with growth in mind.** Focusing on the skills that cannot be taught and allowing for nontraditional candidates who could dynamically improve the organization will help to focus the candidate aperture.

5. **Forgoes acronyms and corporate speak.** Studies show that acronyms and words like "synergy" deter younger job-seekers from applying.[3]

6. **Qualifies the organization's approach to inclusivity and diversity.** Candidates who are looking for a committed, diverse organization will be excited to apply if they see inclusive language in a job description.

Once your team is developing compelling, empathetic job descriptions, encourage them to look at ways to attract a diverse group of candidates. Most states have job boards that focus on diversity hiring with a focus on the differently abled, unemployed, and recently incarcerated.

THE SELECTION PROCESS

Talent acquisition teams are focused on filling positions. Without empathy-forward leadership and proper guidance, the selection process can yield candidates ill-suited to the organization's needs. Remember, the candidate is selecting the organization as much as the organization is selecting the candidate.

From the first conversation, identifying candidate motivations and needs and relating how the organization can meet those needs is key to establishing rapport. The tone should always be open, friendly, and supportive. People show themselves best when they are at ease. The interview process should focus on soft skills as much as hard skills.

Questions for a More Empathetic Interview

- **What would your team members say are your greatest strengths?**

  - "What are your strengths" is a standard interview question. Reframing it in terms of their coworkers' assessment makes the interviewee think about their relationships and interactions.

This can give you insight into how they believe they are perceived and how they relate to the people they work with.

- **Tell me about a difficult work situation and how you overcame it.**

  - This demonstrates problem-solving skills but also gives an understanding of how the candidate dealt with conflict interpersonally. For example, if they immediately escalated to a supervisor, they might be conflict averse, or if the discussion got heated, they might be a hothead.

- **What kind of environment do you work best in?**

  - Understanding the ideal work environment for a candidate can help you understand whether they will perform well in the organization. For example, a person who thrives on a high-energy and collaborative team may struggle as an individual contributor.

- **Describe the accomplishment that makes you most proud.**

  - Give the candidate the opportunity to brag about themselves in a safe space and you will start to unravel their motivations. Digging into *why* they are proud will provide insight into their emotional drivers and what gets them excited about work.

- **How do you react when you are very busy, and a coworker asks you for help?**

  - An individual with a strong empathetic mindset will naturally want to help others. This can help you identify people who are not natural team players but will also show you whether someone could struggle to complete their own tasks. In very collaborative environments, some people struggle to set boundaries with coworkers so they can meet their deadlines.

continued

145

> - **You receive a complaint from a client about a coworker. The client only reached out to you and is not going to escalate the issue. How do you handle it?**
>
>   - This shows if the candidate is capable of constructive, positive peer mentorship. If the candidate immediately escalated to a supervisor, dig deeper. Do they have a fear of confrontation? Was the situation toxic and necessitated higher-level intervention? Were they concerned about retaliation? Understanding how someone reacts in this situation will give insight into how they will interact with the team.

It may be tempting to ask leading questions to identify whether the candidate is culturally a good fit for the organization. An example of a leading question about culture: "We're a fun team here and we like to go out together after work—is that something you'd be comfortable with?" It is best to avoid this line of questioning, as it allows for the possibility of unconscious bias to impede the interview process.

One critical part of interviewing a candidate is building rapport and establishing a connection. Be genuinely interested in the candidate by listening and being fully present. The interview should not be a one-sided grilling but a back-and-forth conversation. Candidates are also judging you and how you feel about your job. They want a manager who is excited, motivated, and enthusiastic about the organization.

AVOIDING BIAS

A lot of organizations talk about "culture fit"—the idea that a candidate should fit into an organization's existing culture. Pride in a positive culture and the desire to hire people who make a positive impact is admirable but can be a dangerous tool if used incorrectly. The unfortunate truth is that despite an increase in diversity and inclusion initiatives, hiring is still heavily influenced by bias.

Studies on Diversity Hiring

- Fifty percent of all employers are less likely to hire obese candidates.[4]
- Resumes with white-sounding names received 50 percent more callbacks.[5]
- Discriminatory hiring practices that disproportionately impact Black and Latinx hiring haven't changed in twenty-five years.[6]
- A gender earnings gap is still prevalent, with women earning 81.1 percent of a man's salary in the same position.[7]

One particularly insidious kind of bias that arises in professional environments across every industry and at every level of success is unconscious bias. Unconscious bias, oftentimes referred to as implicit bias, is prejudice that influences a person's decision making without the person realizing it. This bias occurs automatically, as quick judgments are made based on worldview and past experiences.

Confirmation bias can also be present in an interview process. It is the tendency we have to look for information that supports our opinions and preconceptions. In an interview process, it can lead to favoring candidates who share beliefs, have similar thought processes, or seem more "relatable." Unchecked, this can lead to a homogenized culture and a lack of diverse approaches to solving problems.

There are a few ways to reduce bias in the hiring process, starting with awareness, training, and open discussions. Part of any organization's management training should include a section on understanding, acknowledging, and fighting conscious and unconscious bias. Ensure that the language in your job descriptions is gender neutral and appeals to a broad set of candidates; the screening and interview process is standardized; and all candidates are treated equally. In addition, make the hiring process collaborative, with multiple stakeholders providing feedback.

If you suspect that individuals within your organization cannot be mindful of their biases, blind the resume review process. Eliminate name, age, and any other potentially discriminating information before the manager reviews the resumes.

CLOSING THE CANDIDATE

One of the most frustrating things about the hiring process is when the ideal candidate backs out at the last minute. On its face, the rejection feels unwarranted because time and energy was spent with this candidate getting them ready to take a job that seemed like a good fit for them. Why would they back out now?

The answers vary, but the commonality is that somewhere in the process there was a lack of communication. For example, the talent acquisition team may not have built a strong enough relationship with the candidate and didn't understand the candidate's needs and wants, or the hiring manager may have undersold the position, leaving the candidate second-guessing and feeling hesitant to move forward.

In organizations that look at hiring metrics, the most common reason someone rejects an offer is for a better opportunity. This is an opportunity to leverage the losses to strengthen the organization. Having someone on the hiring team follow up with candidates can help identify areas of improvement. The compensation and benefits may need a refresh, but it's also possible that it's as simple as establishing a better rapport with candidates. Use every loss as an opportunity to do better the next time.

Wrap-up

Hiring can be a challenging undertaking. Applying an empathetic approach to the process gives a better understanding of what the organization needs, as well as a more reliable ability to identify the talent to fill that need. The key elements are—

- Understanding the needs of the organization

- Creating a job description that appeals to a diverse pool of candidates

- Articulating how the role impacts the goals and objectives of the organization

- Maintaining awareness of potential sources of bias while conducting a thorough interview

- Developing a rapport with the candidates to ensure a positive experience and first impression
- Closing the candidate

Chapter 10

Empathetic Marketing Campaigns

START WITH EMPATHY

Think about television commercials that have been especially successful over the years. While some of the most successful are flashy with high production values, others were clearly made on a shoestring budget. Some local ads even get national recognition due to the viral nature of the internet. What is it about those commercials that made them stand out? Empathy.

Without a doubt, marketing is a fundamental catalyst for the growth of most businesses, whether they buy airtime during the Super Bowl or run ads on social media. Marketing is also one of the most effective and time-honored arenas in which to employ empathy. In fact, empathy can have a more significant impact on a marketing campaign than the number of channels, contacts, or funding.

For every successful commercial, there are hundreds that leave no lasting impact. Some even damage their brand by communicating insensitivity and seeming out of touch with the values of their customers. How do these campaigns fail? Whether big or small, the problem is the same: The organization did not understand its customers. And *that* is a failure of empathy.

UNDERSTAND YOUR CUSTOMERS

Understanding your customer is the most critical component of a marketing campaign. Studies have shown that personalized, relevant content appeals to 90 percent of customers.[1] This results in a higher response rate on an ad as well as an overall positive experience with the brand. Conversely, 20 percent of consumers do not trust digital advertising because they find it impersonal and irrelevant, causing a negative perception of a brand and dissuading a potential customer from engaging with it in the future.[2]

> Targeted marketing has been shown to be more effective than market segmentation, and results in a higher response rate and less negative impact to an organization's brand.

To understand customers, start by listening. This can be accomplished in several ways, depending on the resources, the product, and what type of feedback is needed. Some techniques are creating focus groups, soliciting feedback via surveys, or providing free samples of the product for review. However, the most effective strategy also happens to be one everyone can afford: meeting with potential customers.

Salespeople are a valuable resource because they can assist in identifying key attributes of potential customers. Work with the sales team to learn what they hear from the customers. By identifying commonly occurring questions or concerns, the answers to those questions can be built into the marketing content. Discovering the shared experience between customers that drove them to seek out information about the product or service helps shape the narrative of the campaign. Identifying similarities in the demographics and dispositions of customers will also help build a customer profile.

Though conversations with the sales teams will be illuminating, meeting directly with customers and hearing their stories fosters a deeper understanding of their situations. Consider tagging along with the sales team and hear firsthand what customers are saying.

When meeting with potential clients, keep the following questions in mind to capture their responses: What motivates them? What challenges them? What stands between them and their goals? What do they like and dislike about the product? What gets them excited?

Once you have the data, what do you do with it? Many organizations load it into a Customer Relationship Management system with the intention of looking at it when engaging the customer in the future. Often, the data gets forgotten. A better solution is to capture it in a way that helps increase the empathy in your marketing campaign.

An empathy map is a low-cost, easy solution to documenting what customers want.

Empathy Maps

An empathy map is a visualization tool that outlines someone's motivations, behaviors, and opinions. Empathy maps are a common exercise in software development, especially in user interface and user experience engineering. An empathy map helps a development team understand the users' needs, motivations, and challenges, so that development activities meet those needs.

As an example, a car dealership is planning on running an advertising campaign and wants to better understand its customers. The sales team is instructed to construct an empathy map for everyone who enters the dealership. The customer in the following example is fidgety, unhappy, and expresses discontent to the sales associate numerous times during their interaction. He seems indecisive about the car and displays a lack of trust toward the salesperson. After their interaction, the salesperson constructs the empathy map on page 155.

Empathy maps come in several different formats and are easily customizable for different situations. Most maps are divided into quadrants with a circle representing the user at the center. Each quadrant deals with a different aspect of the user: what they say, think, feel, and do. Some empathy maps also include what they hear and see, their challenges, and their goals.

When your employees are meeting with customers, ensure there is a plan in place for them to capture the information they need.

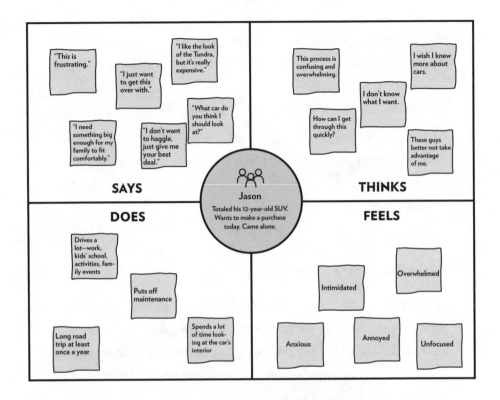

For example, do they have access to records of demographic information and any data gleaned from previous interactions with the customer so they can review this information before the meeting? During meetings, encourage your employees to keep the following questions in mind: What does the customer do and say during the meeting? What factors are influencing them? Who are they listening to? Who do they trust? Some customers will use "I feel" or "I think" statements, but many will not, and it will take asking questions and building an empathy map to clearly understand the customers.

Many times, the boundaries between what a customer thinks and what they feel get cloudy. Employees should record the data on the empathy map regardless and not get hung up on making sure the statements are in the right space. What is important is capturing as much data as possible to construct an empathetic customer profile.

As empathy maps are collected, trends among customers will start to become apparent. Once the marketing team has a solid understanding of the customers, it is time to put that knowledge to use and understand how the product can solve some of the customers' problems.

Be the Customer's Champion

Building an empathetic connection between a product and a customer is as simple as showing the customer how the product addresses their needs. Marketing the product in a dynamic way that evokes an emotional response requires going beyond simply knowing what it is, how it works, and how much it costs.

Knowledge of the features of the product or service is an excellent foundation, but more important is analyzing how those features solve the challenges of the customers. Salespeople should start by collecting data on the features of the product or service, and then compare those features to the data gleaned from conversations with customers. Once those data points are collected, put together a list of features and benefits that speak directly to the customers.

The salespeople in the previous example gathered multiple empathy maps that all told a similar story. While the customers had different reasons for wanting to buy a new car, most of them had the same opinion of the sales process. They lacked trust in the salespeople and felt strong anxiety about making the right decision. Overall, customers do not see buying a car as a pleasant experience. In this case, the focus should be on the process itself. The cars are the same regardless of what dealership is selling them, so the marketing team can gain ground over their competition by advertising an easy sales process. The focus should always be on how your product or service makes your consumers' lives better than your competition does.

Once the data is gathered and compiled, it is time to start building the marketing plan.

CREATE A MARKETING PLAN

All marketing plans should start with an objective. The objective should be something that goes beyond revenue and sales goals and focuses on how the campaign supports and enhances the customer experience. If a cosmetics organization is selling a cutting-edge anti-wrinkle product, the objective should be to help people who care about their wrinkles to see fewer of them. An empathetic marketing plan focuses on how to get the product or service to as many people as possible who will benefit from using it. Always keep the customer in mind and ensure that every decision is in service to them. The sales will come organically if the marketing solves a problem better, cheaper, or faster than the competitors.

Data obtained from the empathy map exercise, or in other interactions with customers, may demonstrate commonalities in their needs. Look for areas of greatest appeal that would have the most impact to someone making a purchase. Focus on what works and show the customer the benefits of the product through relevant and empathetic content.

EMPATHETIC MARKETING CONTENT

Developing empathetic marketing content is an exercise in how the product can be useful to the reader. There is an overwhelming amount of advertising in most people's daily lives. Targeted email campaigns, advertisements on web page banners and sidebars, television commercials, billboards, radio commercials, even ads posing as social media posts all contribute to a constant inundation of targeted and untargeted content. Effective marketing hinges on a strong understanding of what challenges customers are facing, how the product can alleviate those challenges, and what will motivate them to buy something to alleviate those challenges.

The first step in developing dynamic marketing content is to stop selling. This may seem counterintuitive, but pushing the product is the job of your sales team. The marketing content is to get the customer excited about what their life will be like after the product changes it. Think about the advertisements that resulted in you making a purchase. More than likely, you decided to buy because you saw someone solve a problem like one you were experiencing. You empathized. You were hooked.

A narrative-driven campaign will fundamentally change how a consumer relates to the product on a biological level. There is a physiological difference between reading a product description and reading a story. Reading fiction makes lasting impacts on the structure of the brain itself.[3] The same parts of the brain are stimulated when hearing or reading about an event and taking part in the event itself. A narrative-driven advertisement stays with a consumer longer and gets them more engaged physically and emotionally.

Effective, empathetic marketing evokes emotion. A successful marketing campaign relies on empathizing with customers, but a truly impactful campaign will result in emotional buy-in from the customer.

Stories can have a drastic impact on a marketing campaign. A story takes the focus off selling the product and puts it on the customer. This is where the data from the empathy map really shines, tying together the common threads and allowing a customer to see themselves reflected in the marketing content.

An often-employed strategy is to turn an existing customer into a hero and let them tell the story themself.

The Customer Hero

A customer hero story is something that puts a customer front and center, focusing on how the experience of using the product changed their situation.

One of the earliest examples of a customer hero story is a commercial that aired during the 1984 Super Bowl. Apple ran the advertisement as an attack on IBM.[4] In the commercial, IBM is portrayed as a faceless and oppressive organization. The commercial does not detail much about Apple's new product, except to suggest that it will disrupt the status quo. Many people saw IBM as a company with an oppressive monopoly, and the commercial resonated due to its provocative nature. The woman in the commercial was a hero without ever having to mention a benefit or feature of the product.

The first step to building a customer hero story is to identify a customer who has experienced a positive outcome from using the product or service and is willing to share their experience. Ask the sales teams for individuals who have been the most effusive after a sale. If they have been following the advice in Chapter 11 about Selling with Empathy, they should be regularly following up with their customers after a sale to see how things are going.

Once you have found a customer willing to share their story, or ideally a few customers willing to share their stories, ask them to walk through their entire experience: their situation before the product; the experience of finding the product; their experience with buying the product; what it was like the first time they used it; what their experience is now.

Take that information and craft it into a narrative from their perspective. Tell a story of how the product changed their life. That story should help form the foundation of the marketing campaign.

It is also powerful to advertise actual testimonials from customers via print or video, as demonstrated in the following situation.

Word of Mouth

Louis had recently purchased a new house in a new city where he did not know many people. Before he moved in, he wanted to have the interior of the house painted. This was his first house, and he was nervous about being taken advantage of. He searched online for local painters and visited each of their websites individually. He was on a limited budget and intended to use a smaller organization or a local painter to save money, but most of the websites he visited left him nervous. The services and prices all looked similar, but nothing stood out to overcome his nervousness.

The final website he went to had a section called "Customer Testimonials" and included a series of videos of customers who had their homes or businesses painted. The videos weren't flashy, and they were taken from a cell phone camera without professional staging. Video after video showed satisfied customers, a few of whom expressed they had similar concerns that were overcome by the professionalism and transparency of the painters. Louis chose this organization because he felt a level of connection with the customers and wanted to experience the same level of satisfaction that they had.

The Lesson: People respond well to being told a story where they identify with the protagonist. Crafting narratives that demonstrate the capability of the product from the customer's perspective is extremely powerful and compelling.

ADVERTISE

Now that you have a strong understanding of the customers, the product or service, and have a strong compelling narrative, it is time to market the product. How you decide to go about this will depend on the kind of resources available. Often when launching a new product, funding is limited, so now is the time to get creative.

Start simple and market to existing customers. Look at the database of clients and contacts. Is there overlap with the target demographic? Can current relationships be used to turn customers into repeat customers for this new product or service?

Think about the target demographic identified during the understanding-the-customer phase. Ask what publications they read, what they watch, and what they listen to. What medium will reach your customers quickly and effectively?

Turn employees into marketers. The adage that everyone is in sales is just as true for marketing. Teach the employees about the product and encourage them to network. Reward them for qualified leads.

Develop content for social media and blogs, start conversations on relevant posts, display the product at conferences, or send experts on to panels to speak and contribute to conversations.

Grassroots marketing is challenging, but if the story is compelling, there will be an audience for it. Think about the number of small, rural advertising pieces that have gone viral because they were especially creative, interesting, or emotional. What do most of them have in common? They told a story that made people empathize.

REVIEW AND REPEAT

Even following all the advice in this chapter, the marketing campaign may not be as effective as hoped. Especially marketing a new product to a new audience. There are many variables that influence someone to buy. Break down the campaign and look at what worked and what did not. Maybe both online and print ads were run. Was one significantly more successful than the other? Can resources be reallocated to the successful avenues to make them more impactful? Is there anything to do to make the less successful channels more successful?

Wrap-up

Marketing is a fundamental catalyst for the growth of most businesses and is also one of the most effective and time-honored arenas in which to employ empathy. In fact, empathy can have a more significant impact on a marketing campaign than the number of channels, contacts, or funding. Goals to keep in mind for a successful empathetic marketing campaign include the following:

- Craft the campaign with empathy for the customer at the forefront.

- Strive to understand the customers and use tools like empathy maps to better conceptualize their needs.

- Create a marketing plan.

- Create empathetic marketing content by teaching customers about how their lives can be improved by the product or service.

- Advertise, review the results, and innovate new content.

Chapter 11

Selling with Empathy

WHY IS EMPATHY IMPORTANT IN SALES?

Empathy is critical in any organization's sales strategy. Understanding a potential customer's genuine wants and needs dramatically increases the likelihood of a successful sale. In a study conducted by Caliper, only 55 percent of salespeople have the right personality traits to be successful. They discovered that many lack a key component required to be effective: empathy.[1]

Empathy allows for a deeper understanding of someone's motivations and helps you to see a situation as someone else sees it. The best sales approach feels like a partnership by providing a good or service to someone who needs it to help them achieve goals they could not otherwise achieve. The surest way to convert a prospect into a customer is to work with them to solve an issue with a product or service that you provide.

Without understanding the customer's needs, you are not in charge of the sale. You may get lucky, they may still buy a car, but you are not responsible for that sale. Being in control of the sale requires empathy with the customer. Seeing the situation from the customer's perspective, and understanding their needs, motivations, and challenges, drastically increases sales. The sales pitch can be targeted based on that information and guide the customer to buying the product or service. Effective empathy-based sales campaigns begin with the first contact and continue beyond the close.

EMPATHIZE WITH THE CUSTOMER

Getting to know a customer takes time, but it is an imperative part of any sales process. Although there are a few ways to coax information out of potential customers, the most effective sales techniques are born from a genuine desire to help the customer. While some salespeople are adept enough to fake it, it is more effective to genuinely believe that the product or service has value to a customer.

Understanding or relating to someone's experiences and validating their emotions create an authentic connection. There are a few strategies to employ to engender those feelings of connection with another person.

It's important to make people comfortable when working to establish a bond. A commonly employed technique in putting a person at ease is voice mirroring. This is a conversational technique whereby a person matches the cadence and speech patterns of the person to whom they are speaking. If the person speaks formally, respond in kind. If they are more laid back, use more casual language. People tend to feel more comfortable with people who sound like them and they are immediately more relaxed and receptive.

Voice mirroring is not the same as copying the vocabulary of the person being mirrored. Think about a time you have witnessed an adult try to use youthful slang to artificially bond with a teenager. Does it usually go over well? Rarely. That is because the adult is using language they are not comfortable with. It often comes across as awkward and stilted. Voice mirroring is not about mimicry, it is about modifying the formality and cadence of speech. If the idea of changing communication styles to fit the customer seems challenging, consider role playing with people of varied and diverse backgrounds. Be sure to remain authentic throughout this process. Mastering the art of voice mirroring helps immensely in feeling comfortable selling to anyone.

Once the customer is at ease, ask leading questions and actively listen to the customer's responses. Slow down, be present, and stop the hard sell. Query them about their current experiences, their challenges, their needs, and how they feel about the possibility of a solution. This last part is especially important. Understanding how a customer feels about their situation gives insight into their readiness and willingness to change it. The more critical the situation, the more they need the product or service. Please refer to Appendix E for more detailed information on how to effectively apply voice mirroring.

THE VALUE OF COMMUNICATION

Once a bond has been developed with the customer, it's time to begin the sales pitch. The more bonded and connected to a customer, the more influence the salesperson has. The key to a good sale is to avoid pushing too hard, show interest in the customer as a human being, and keep the focus on solving the customer's problem.

But what if there is no ability to build a one-on-one relationship, and the sales must start with cold calling? It takes an average of eight cold-call attempts to reach someone. Make it count. Stop thinking in terms of making a sale and start thinking about building a relationship. Before making a call, make a plan.

In all successful relationships, communication, honesty, and support are present. A typical strategy for call plans is to make initial contact and then follow up periodically every few months. The likelihood of building a substantive relationship with someone through intermittent contact is low. Find a balance between reaching out too often and taking so long between tag-ups that they forget who you are. In any relationship, intermittent conversations with multiple-month gaps are unlikely to result in a bond. Continue to focus on providing a benefit to the other person every time you talk. It could be advice, it could be introducing them to a valuable connection, it could be a small present, something to hook them so that you are the first person they think of when they need to make a purchase. Networking events, wine tastings, and other events that are socially focused will also help to build rapport.

Evolve the sales pitch and refine it based on the things that are most pressing to the customers. Use the experience gained over time to look at trends for people in similar situations (demographically by industry, title, etc.) to assess common challenges and motivators.

In-person and phone conversations are always preferable for sales pitches, but there are times that email is the only way to reach a customer. People receive dozens, if not hundreds, of unsolicited emails a day, so think about how to truly make them effective. If you know the customer, it is easy to craft an email to stand out from the rest.

If you have ever received a sales email from a car dealer, you know that many of them are similar: a subject line advertising a sales event, several car pictures, and a few descriptions that may or may not match what you are looking for. Those kinds of emails are designed to appeal to as many people as possible to lure them into the showroom. Bulk emails can be impactful if they are specific to a smaller group and customized to address a commonality in each of the recipients. If the salesperson followed the preceding advice, they would have a strong knowledge of the customer and be able to target their sales emails appropriately.

If you have ever bought a car from a dealership, you've probably ended up on their marketing email distribution list. Consider a standard Fourth of July sales event email. They all follow the same basic formula: eye-catching reds and blues, and pictures of car models that are on sale for low, low prices. Compare that to the following email, where a salesperson takes a more personal approach to selling a car during a sales event.

Subject Line: How was Myrtle Beach?

Hi Brian,

I hope you're doing well and handling this heat wave! Last time we spoke you were taking the kids down to Myrtle Beach for a vacation—how was it? I got down to the Outer Banks for a long weekend and the weather sucked. Rained the entire time. Isn't that always how it is

continued

when you finally take a vacation?? Hope your beach time was better than mine!

I know you had some hesitation about buying last time you came by, but I wanted to let you know that we're having a 4th of July sale this weekend and the model you were interested in is going to be part of it. You'd be looking at about $3,000 cash back and I could swing a better deal on your trade-in. I know when we talked last it was not the right time, but I did not want you to miss out on this. It's a really good deal.

Let me know what you're thinking. If it's still not the right time, no problem, I'll keep you posted as we have other sales or offers on the Ultima. Take care, talk soon.

This email is significantly less formal, and for good reason. This customer conducted himself informally, spoke informally, and seemed to respond well to informal language when the salesperson mirrored his speech. Phrases like "the weather sucked" will seem completely unprofessional and unacceptable to some people, and for good reason. However, if you had a negative reaction to that phrase, examine it. What makes you uncomfortable about speaking to a customer that way? Is your discomfort born from a dislike of that word or is it because you were trained not to use informal language? One of those is an authentic value, the other is a learned behavior. If you are uncomfortable because of your training, examine whether that still holds up in today's market.

Nowadays, sales happen everywhere and through every communication medium: in person, at bars, via email, even via text message. The generation reaching buying age now grew up on digital platforms and is more comfortable with slang than formal speech. The point is: Target your sales communications to the individual. Adjust the tone, phrasing, and language accordingly. Be authentic and do not use language you are not comfortable with, because it is transparent when you do. However, if you are familiar with a customer and feel a sense of connection, use it to your advantage.

SALES MEETINGS

Some sales opportunities necessitate meetings where the sales pitch is to a room full of people. The customer may need buy-in from other stakeholders, may not be the decision maker, or may want to collaborate with others before making a decision. It may not be possible to identify everyone's contribution to the decision. Some salespeople try to ask questions about reporting lines and understand the complex interpersonal dynamics within an organization. This is a waste of energy. The goal of the meeting, regardless of reporting structure, is to have every person present walking away wanting the product or service. If there is enough lead time, and the customer is willing to make introductions to the meeting participants before the meeting, do the work beforehand. Learn about each of the participants by applying the techniques in the previous section.

Often, there is not the time or ability to have those conversations before the meeting. In those cases, engage with everyone in the room to understand what they need and ask questions to better understand the evaluation criteria they are using to make a buying decision. Work to understand what their responses are saying. Listen actively, and work with individuals on their concerns, challenges, and needs in real time. This will not only demonstrate knowledge of the product, but it will also endear you to everyone.

CLOSING

There is a lot of pressure on a salesperson to close, both from their leadership and from themselves. Sometimes a sale can be the difference between paying bills on time and missing a mortgage payment. However, do not underestimate the amount of pressure on the customer: pressure from supervisors, pressure from stakeholders, even internal pressure to make the right decision.

If the customer must escalate the decision to superiors to get approval to purchase, ensure they are armed with a strong pitch. Coach them on how to sell the product to their supervisor. Walk through the conversation with them. What kinds of questions does the supervisor typically ask in these situations? Will they be focused on the product features? Focused on the return on investment (ROI)? Or will it just be about the cost? Try to understand their internal processes and procedures to ensure that the sales process syncs up with the customer's needs for a decision.

FOLLOW UP

What if, despite a great effort, the customer decides not to buy? Record the customer information so if they return, there is a place to start. Capturing the customer's contact information gives the opportunity to reach out to them in the future with a customized and personal communication. Collecting notes on customers throughout the sales process can help immensely at all stages, but especially during the follow-up. Simple, personal steps can go a long way toward getting repeat business.

Regardless of whether the customer bought the good or service, conduct a "lessons learned" exercise. This provides the opportunity to identify strengths and weaknesses in both the sales approach and sales pitch. It may even give insight into improvements to make the product or service more appealing to customers. Dig in, find out why the customer made the decision they made, and solicit honest, thorough feedback. Even in a successful sale, there is room for improvement and opportunities to learn.

If the customer did buy, do not underestimate the importance of following up. Even if the product or service is a one-time transaction, the act of reengaging with them within the first month of selling the product is powerful. Find out what they like about it as well as what could be improved. Ask them to critique the sales pitch and find out if they felt comfortable throughout the process. Finally, see if the customer knows of any referrals who could benefit from the product.

One caution—leading with a request for referrals is making the situation about what you need. By letting the customer share their experience, provide critiques, and talk through their feelings they will be more likely to share their contacts. Some of the most lucrative clients are ones that help you grow your contact list because they benefited from the product.

Wrap-up

....

An empathetic sales approach ensures increased close rates, better relationships with clients, and more repeat business. The keys to a successful sales strategy are as follows:

- Get to know your customers and understand their needs.

- Refine your pitch based on what you learn from customers.

- Develop a targeted communication strategy for potential and returning customers.

- Capitalize on sales meetings.

- Follow up to understand what is working and what needs to improve.

Chapter 12

Key Takeaways

"Empathy is the ability to understand and relate to an individual's emotional state, motivations, and needs while reserving judgment and remaining neutral."

Why Is Empathy Important in the Workplace? Empathy is a cornerstone of leadership excellence in addressing many of the challenges facing organizations today. It is a hard commercial tool that every business needs for low attrition and high customer satisfaction.

Empathy Is Low Cost, High Return. There is no simple formula to determine the direct return on empathy. However, the increases in sales, customer engagement, and employee productivity are measurable and improve when the management team is empathetic.

ORGANIZATIONAL STRENGTH THROUGH EMPATHY

Building Strong Organizations. People are the cornerstone of any organization. Motivating and engaging them is critical to ensure the success of the business. People work best when they understand the leader's vision and feel connected to their managers. Leadership sets the tone for the organization; positive, engaged, and empathetic leaders inspire people to do their best work.

High-Performance Teams. Building and developing high-performance teams takes empathetic leadership and the ability to see individual strengths and weaknesses. An empathetic leader puts people in positions where they can be successful based on their unique contributions. A team that is focused on specific, achievable goals and whose members feel strong connections to their management and one another will accomplish great things.

Diversity and Inclusion. Diversity and inclusion are the foundation of a healthy and robust organization. Diversity of thought creates space for unique and inventive solutions to problems. Addressing fears and biases toward people of different backgrounds and embracing diversity makes the organization stronger.

MANAGING AND LEADING WITH EMPATHY

Management Styles and Empathy. Each of the four basic management styles—autocratic, democratic, laissez-faire, and nurturing—can be used empathetically and effectively. A good leader knows how to alternate between these management styles, depending on the situation, team, or individual they are leading.

Leadership with Empathy. Empathetic and effective leaders must know themselves, boost empathy, empower their team, maximize individual strengths, and motivate and inspire.

Developing Empathetic Communication Techniques. Empathetic communication techniques are critical to good leadership. Effective, authentic, and truthful communication improves productivity and morale; reduces absenteeism and turnover rates; and increases employees' efficiency, productivity, and feeling of being valued.

Effective Confrontation through Empathy. Empathetic confrontation creates a common vision going forward by presenting the issues in a way that reduces emotion for both parties. The goal of empathetic confrontation is not to produce separation but rather to create unity. The most effective confrontation is one in which emotions and ego are put aside and the discussion centers on how to solve the issue.

Managing Empathetically during Transformation or Change. One of the most difficult times to manage people is during a change or transformation. Many people will resist any change, even if they know it is for good. As a result, building trust is one of the most effective ways to manage change. Fostering trust allows for sharing of information, feelings, and opinions. This open line of communication gives leaders a chance to better understand the people they lead, building relationships and creating a stronger workplace community in the process.

GROWING A BUSINESS THROUGH EMPATHETIC LEADERSHIP

Empathy and Hiring. Every organization is unique, and each has a set of priorities and challenges requiring a customized approach to achieve success. Understanding what is needed is the first step in attracting a team of individuals to execute the vision. Applying an empathy-based approach to hiring is a proven method to ensure the organization has the right people in the right positions. Break the mold and shake up antiquated and biased hiring practices and you will see a significant increase in your teams' productivity and cohesiveness.

Empathetic Marketing Campaigns. Regardless of the product or service, the organization is solving a problem for someone. Engaging with potential customers by creating relatable, targeted content takes an in-depth understanding of what people need.

Selling with Empathy. Understanding the customer's fears and challenges provides a unique opportunity. Nobody enjoys receiving a sales call, but most people will listen to a pitch if it clearly can solve a problem they are experiencing. Customizing and targeting communication through the entire sales process will result in higher customer engagement and better relationships.

THE BOTTOM LINE

Empathy is a must-have for any organization looking to reduce attrition, increase customer satisfaction, and make a positive impact on the lives of its team members and clients.

Everyone who interacts with you is a complex individual with unique and personal needs. Showing them empathy is a zero-cost solution to alleviate dissatisfaction in the workforce.

Empathy isn't about caving to someone's needs or making excuses for someone's behavior. It's about building relationships that drive and define a business and about approaching all aspects of leadership openly and empathetically.

Empathetic leaders are driving their businesses into the future by applying the practical, low-cost solutions found in this book. Making a significant change in your situation starts with one person: You.

Acknowledgments

To Tina's husband, Jay, who provided support and encouragement during the writing process.

To Neal's friend Jocelyn, who red-penned his early drafts and never pulled her punches.

To Tina's writer's group, who kept her writing and entertained.

To Neal's parents for their support and patience over the years.

To Kate, Toni, Astrid, Bill, Andy, Lisa, and Chris, who helped us become better leaders.

Appendix A

Manager Type Checklist

The four leadership styles that follow have been partially adapted from studies in the 1930s by Kurt Lewin, who proposed the first framework on leadership styles.

THE AUTOCRATIC MANAGER

Autocratic Manager Characteristics:

- The manager retains authority and receives little input from any team member
- The team is expected to obey orders without the need for explanation
- Motivation is typically through a structured set of rewards and punishments

The Autocratic Style Is Effective When:

- Decision-making time is limited

- Quick, organized action is essential

- Executing rapid change

- Team members do not understand tasks, procedures, or priorities

Mismanagement of Autocratic Style:

- Unwillingness to listen to employees

- Blaming and diminishing employees

- Withholding information

- Inappropriate behavior (e.g., sexual and racial harassment)

- Lack of respect toward employees

- Bullying or creating a fear-based environment

- Micromanaging, creating an environment of mistrust

Managing with Empathy as an Autocratic Manager:

- Watch over employees' mental and emotional well-being

- Positively recognize members, show appreciation for their value

THE DEMOCRATIC MANAGER

Democratic Manager Characteristics:

- Encourages all stakeholders to participate in the decision-making process
- Keeps their team members and stakeholders informed about everything that affects their work
- Shares decision-making and problem-solving responsibilities
- Delegates authority to staff

The Democratic Style Is Effective When:

- The team is highly skilled or experienced
- Implementing operational changes
- Resolving group problems
- A large or complex problem requires input from many people for its solution

Mismanagement of the Democratic Style:

- Lack of decision making
- Wanting to please everyone and being indecisive
- Making decisions based on the needs of the most vocal employee

Managing with Empathy as a Democratic Manager:

- Actively seek input from team members

- Listen to employees and involve employees to support the problem solving and decision making

- Employ a coaching technique

THE LAISSEZ-FAIRE MANAGER

Laissez-Faire Manager Characteristics:

- Manager provides little or no direction and gives employees as much freedom as possible

- Employees must determine their own goals, make decisions, and resolve problems on their own

The Laissez-Faire Style Is Effective When:

- Team members are highly skilled and experienced

- Team members are willing and able to make decisions for the success of the organization

- The roles and responsibilities are clear

- The employees know their roles; little change is expected in time frames or constraints

Mismanagement of the Laissez-Faire Style:

- Manager may evade the duties of management
- Unwillingness to listen to employees
- Favoritism
- Lack of decision making
- Inability to get engaged

Managing with Empathy as a Laissez-Faire Manager:

- Focus on the vision, expertise, and enthusiasm
- Pay attention to the employees and provide encouragement; make sure people feel they are valued members of the team

THE NURTURING MANAGER

Nurturing Manager Characteristics:

- The manager cares for, nurtures, and proactively takes responsibility to support others
- Encourages open and honest communication
- Respects employees and coworkers
- Fosters the organization's sense of community

- Team members exhibit a sense of belonging to "a good team." This style keeps employee attrition low.

The Nurturing Style Is Effective:

- When it is critical to keep employees happy and bonded together
- When employees need a sense of community (field or remote personnel)

Mismanagement of the Nurturing Style:

- Lack of decision making (not wanting to alienate people or risk having someone dislike them)
- Conflict avoidance
- Decisions based only on employee well-being (and not necessarily what is best for the organization as a whole)
- Favoritism

Managing with Empathy as a Nurturing Manager:

- Actively respect employees and create a sense of community
- Encourage communication
- Broad-based delegation, and trust
- Team members believe they are cared for

Appendix B

Confrontation Steps

EMPATHETIC CONFRONTATION: STEPS TOWARD SUCCESS

This guide contains the practical steps to help you set up the calm, detached approach that fosters empathetic and productive confrontation.

- **Determine a common goal for the meeting.** Make sure the meeting is only about this goal. Confrontation is about helping the other person and resolving a specific issue. Keep your mind on resolving the issue—not berating the other person or making them feel bad. The less emotion brought to the discussion, the better.

- **Do not make a play for the other person's emotions.** Most people do not care what you feel, think, or believe—especially when they feel uneasy and stressed themselves. Focus the discussion on the issue. Do not bring in your anger, fear, or ego. This is about the other person and not about you. This is not the time to try to get sympathy (e.g., "your performance is making me look bad"); to vent your anger to make yourself feel better; or to be arrogant and state how much better you could do their work.

- **Make sure you understand your own reactions.** What are you invested in? What are you reacting to? Why are you angry? What are your motivators? Being right? Doing things your way? Making everyone on the team happy? Remember that in the vast majority of cases, even when it seems that someone is attacking you, they're usually only protecting themselves from a perceived threat.

- **Find a way to help the other person save face.** Saving face means preserving "self-esteem, self-worth, identity, reputation, status, pride, and dignity."[1] This means respecting the individual and being willing to give the other person a way to renegotiate their position to preserve their dignity. It is detrimental during confrontation to cause shame, fear, and anger in others. This breaks down trust and creates a fear-based environment.

- **Tackle the underlying issues and not the behavior.** Figure out why they are acting the way they do by asking questions, listening to them, and figuring out the root cause.

- **Do not presume to know what they think.** Avoid asserting that you understand the other person or their position on the issue. The reality is that you almost never have the whole picture—especially from another person's perspective—only what they choose to share with you.

- **Present constructive options to the individual you are confronting.** Creating a respectful way out of confrontation is an act of great maturity and enlightened, empathetic leadership. Be careful, however, to avoid providing choices you do not have the ability to follow through on, that you do not really agree with, or that you know the other person would not agree to.

Appendix C

Managing Transformation Guide

STEPS FOR MANAGING A TRANSFORMATION

1. **Create a vision and goals.** Have a vision and organizational goals that can be articulated clearly and easily. The vision provides a framework around which to make decisions.

2. **Create a plan that translates the vision into actionable steps.** Create a step-by-step list of activities and a schedule for the transformation. It is critical to have actionable and clear steps in the plan. Bring in stakeholders to review the plan. Put in resources and costs for each activity to make it clear to all stakeholders the transformation costs in time, resources, and opportunity. Opportunity costs are tasks not done while the team is working on the transformation. It is important to be

flexible and agile during the transformation process, but the steps provide a framework for the team to go about implementing the transformation.

3. **Create a team of people who are champions of the change.** The champions can be stakeholders, members of the staff, or anyone to help with the plan. The process improvement team is a great starting point in creating a team of champions from different parts of the project or organization. Once that team understands the vision and the necessity for the transformation, they can evangelize and communicate the change across the organization.

4. **Develop a communication plan to give frequent and regular updates to the whole team.** It is critically important to over-communicate to anyone affected by the transformation. Provide regular updates and be honest on what is working and what needs to be adjusted.

5. **Have a retrospective every week.** Be honest and go through what is working and what is not working in the transformation process. Recognize any disgruntled people and plan to provide additional communication to them.

Appendix D

Job Description Guide

Job Title

- Use job titles that are specific to your position and that will stand out against titles that are overused.

- Avoid overly clever names and titles that appear gimmicky.

General Guidance

- Eliminate pronouns from your description and make the job description gender neutral.

- Replace gender-coded words (e.g., "rock star" or "salesman") with neutral words.

- Avoid acronyms and corporate speak.

Job Responsibilities

- Include a strong, attention-grabbing summary at the top: Why are you looking and why is the opportunity an exciting one?

- Articulate what aspects of the role, team, or organization are unique.

- Add a "day-in-the-life" section with specific information about tasks and responsibilities.

- Include milestones and define success in the role.

Job Requirements

- Identify the bare minimum of skills required to do the job.

- Focus on behavioral qualities that will make someone successful in the role.

- Avoid overly complicated job descriptions with laundry list requirements.

Culture and Values

- Qualify your organization's approach to diversity and inclusion.

- Take the time to articulate your organization's culture and how you view employee well-being.

Call to Action

- End the post by encouraging candidates to apply, and reinforce how excited your organization is to be looking for new talent.

Appendix E

Mirroring Guide

VOICE MIRRORING

Voice mirroring is a conversational technique whereby a person matches the cadence and speech patterns of the person to whom they are speaking. People feel more comfortable with people who sound like them and they are immediately more relaxed and receptive.

When someone...	You...
Speaks formally and reservedly	Refrain from using colloquialisms Keep your language formal and unemotional
Speaks casually with varied inflection	Match their enthusiasm and cadence Use smaller, less-formal words
Uses anecdotes or analogies frequently	Repeat back to them to correlate between their stories and the point they were making Tell your own stories
Speaks in short, direct sentences	Deliver points succinctly Refrain from elaboration and colorful language

An important note: Avoid mocking someone's speech pattern. Do not copy their accent or use the exact same language or it will come off as disingenuous. For example, if someone uses colloquial vocatives (man, buddy, pal, etc.), do not use the same one. Use one you're comfortable with so it sounds natural.

POSITION MIRRORING

Position mirroring is the act of moving your body to sync your posture and position with the person you're speaking to. This can work for posture as well as gestures.

When someone...	You...
Crosses their arms	Wait for 30 to 60 seconds and cross your arms
Shifts in their chair	Adjust your own sitting position
Leans back in their chair	Lean forward casually
Clasps their hands	Fold your hands in a similar manner
Punctuates sentences by pointing	Point when making a statement you want to accentuate

An important note: Do not try to mirror someone exactly or the other person will notice. The idea is to notice gestures that the other person makes and make similar, but not exact, motions of your own. Discreet, asynchronous movement is key.

Notes

PREFACE

1. Harter, Jim. "U.S. Employee Engagement Reverts Back to Pre-Covid-19 Levels." Gallup, January 21, 2022. https://www.gallup.com/workplace/321965/employee-engagement-reverts-back-pre-covid-levels.aspx.

2. Harter, Jim. "U.S. Employee Engagement Reverts Back to Pre-Covid-19 Levels." Gallup, January 21, 2022. https://www.gallup.com/workplace/321965/employee-engagement-reverts-back-pre-covid-levels.aspx.

3. Andrews, Ryan. "One Word Is the Solution to America's $600 Billion Productivity Drain." LinkedIn, March 9, 2018. https://www.linkedin.com/pulse/one-word-solution-americas-600-billion-productivity-drain-andrews.

4. Parmar, Belinda. "Corporate Empathy Is Not an Oxymoron." *Harvard Business Review*, January 8, 2015. https://hbr.org/2015/01/corporate-empathy-is-not-an-oxymoron.

5. Parmar, Belinda. "Corporate Empathy Is Not an Oxymoron." *Harvard Business Review*, January 8, 2015. https://hbr.org/2015/01/corporate-empathy-is-not-an-oxymoron.

6. "Empathy (n.)." Etymology. Online Etymology Dictionary. Accessed April 21, 2022. http://www.etymonline.com/word/empathy.

7. Lanzoni, Susan. "A Short History of Empathy." Atlantic Media Company, October 15, 2015. https://www.theatlantic.com/health/archive/2015/10/a-short-history-of-empathy/409912/.

8. "Anterior Cingulate Cortex." Wikipedia. April 4, 2022. https://en.wikipedia.org/wiki/Anterior_cingulate_cortex.

9. Winerman, Lea. "The Mind's Mirror." Monitor on Psychology. American Psychological Association, October 2005. https://www.apa.org/monitor/oct05/mirror.

10. Marsh, Jason. "Do Mirror Neurons Give Us Empathy?" *Greater Good Magazine*, March 29, 2012. https://greatergood.berkeley.edu/article/item/do_mirror_neurons_give_empathy.

INTRODUCTION

1. "The Deloitte Global 2021 Millennial and Gen Z Survey." Deloitte, 2021. https://www2.deloitte.com/global/en/pages/about-deloitte/articles/millennialsurvey.html.

2. "State of Workplace Empathy." Businessolver. https://www.businessolver.com/resources/state-of-workplace-empathy.

3. "State of Workplace Empathy." Businessolver. https://www.businessolver.com/resources/state-of-workplace-empathy.

CHAPTER 1

1. "State of Workplace Empathy." Businessolver. https://www.businessolver.com/resources/state-of-workplace-empathy.

CHAPTER 2

1. Larson, Erik. "New Research: Diversity + Inclusion = Better Decision Making at Work." *Forbes Magazine*, September 21, 2017. https://www.forbes.com/sites/eriklarson/2017/09/21/new-research-diversity-inclusion-better-decision-making-at-work/#5317a9824cbf.

2. Larson, Erik. "New Research: Diversity + Inclusion = Better Decision Making at Work." *Forbes Magazine*, September 21, 2017. https://www.forbes.com/sites/eriklarson/2017/09/21/new-research-diversity-inclusion-better-decision-making-at-work/#5317a9824cbf.

CHAPTER 3

1. Travis, Nigel. *The Challenge Culture: Why the Most Successful Organizations Run on Pushback* (New York: Hachette Book Group, 2018), 100.

2. Useem, Jerry. "Power Causes Brain Damage." Atlantic Media Company, June 23, 2017. https://www.theatlantic.com/magazine/archive/2017/07/power-causes-brain-damage/528711/.

3. David Owen and Jonathan Davidson, "Hubris Syndrome: An Acquired Personality Disorder? A Study of US Presidents and UK Prime Ministers over the Last 100 Years," *Brain* 132, no. 5 (May 2009): 1396–1406; https://doi.org/10.1093/brain/awp008.

4. El-Attrash, Francesca. "How to Embrace Diversity with Empathy." GovLoop, June 3, 2020. https://www.govloop.com/embrace-diversity-empathy/.

5. "How to Identify Hidden Biases." Careercast.com Diversity Network, February 14, 2017. https://diversity.careercast.com/article/how-identify-hidden-biases.

6. WomensMedia. "Act Now To Shrink the Confidence Gap." *Forbes Magazine*, April 28, 2014. https://www.forbes.com/sites/womensmedia/2014/04/28/act-now-to-shrink-the-confidence-gap/?sh=684bff295c41.

CHAPTER 5

1. Freedman, Joshua. "Tough Empathy: Head + Heart." LinkedIn, June 9, 2014. https://www.linkedin.com/pulse/20140609204214-198001-tough-empathy-head-heart/.

2. Nadella, Satya. Vanity Fair's New Establishment Summit, 2017, Los Angeles, Calif.

CHAPTER 6

1. Mehrabian, Albert. *Silent Messages*, (Belmont, CA: Wadsworth Publishing Company, 1972).

2. Power, Rhett. "5 Signs Someone Is Lying to You." *Inc.*, August 5, 2015. https://www.inc.com/rhett-power/5-signs-someone-is-lying-to-you.html.

CHAPTER 7

1. Richard, Skip. "Saving Face: How to Preserve Dignity and Build Trust." Skip Prichard | Leadership Insights, June 16, 2020. https://www.skipprichard.com/saving-face-how-to-preserve-dignity-and-build-trust/.

CHAPTER 8

1. Morgan, Blake. "10 Examples of How Covid-19 Forced Business Transformation." *Forbes Magazine*, May 1, 2020. https://www.forbes.com/sites/blakemorgan/2020/05/01/10-examples-of-how-covid-19-forced-business-transformation/?sh=717475d41be3.

CHAPTER 9

1. "State of Workplace Empathy." Businessolver. https://www.businessolver.com/resources/state-of-workplace-empathy.

2. Mohr, Tara Sophia. "Why Women Don't Apply for Jobs Unless They're 100% Qualified." *Harvard Business Review*, August 25, 2014. https://hbr.org/2014/08/why-women-dont-apply-for-jobs-unless-theyre-100-qualified.

3. Huppert, Maxwell. "Cut the Jargon, and 3 Other Tips for Entry-Level Job Descriptions." Business Solutions on LinkedIn, December 13, 2017. https://business.linkedin.com/talent-solutions/blog/job-descriptions/2017/cut-the-jargon-and-3-other-tips-for-entry-level-job-description.

4. Bevan, Stephen. "50% Of All Employers Are Less Likely to Hire Obese Candidates." World Economic Forum, February 6, 2019. https://www.weforum.org/agenda/2019/02/half-of-employers-say-they-are-less-inclined-to-recruit-obese-candidates-its-not-ok/.

5. Bertrand, Marianne, and Sendhil Mullainathan. "Discrimination in the Job Market in the United States." The Abdul Latif Jameel Poverty Action Lab (J-PAL), 2004. https://www.povertyactionlab.org/evaluation/discrimination-job-market-united-states.

6. Lopez, German. "Study: Anti-Black Hiring Discrimination Is as Prevalent Today as It Was in 1989." Vox, September 18, 2017. https://www.vox.com/identities/2017/9/18/16307782/study-racism-jobs.

7. Hegewisch, Ariane, and Heidi Hartmann. "The Gender Wage Gap: 2018 Earnings Differences by Race and Ethnicity." Institute for Women's Policy Research, March 7, 2019. https://iwpr.org/iwpr-issues/esme/the-gender-wage-gap-by-occupation-2018/.

CHAPTER 10

1. "The Power of Me: The Impact of Personalization on Marketing Performance." SlideShare, a Scribd company, January 4, 2018. https://www.slideshare.net/EpsilonMktg/the-power-of-me-the-impact-of-personalization-on-marketing-performance/1.

2. Morrison, Kimberlee. "Consumers Don't like and Don't Trust Digital Advertising (Infographic)." Adweek, May 5, 2017. http://www.adweek.com/digital/consumers-dont-like-and-dont-trust-digital-advertising-infographic/.

3. Clark, Carol. "A Novel Look at How Stories May Change the Brain." eScienceCommons. Emory University, December 17, 2013. https://news.emory.edu/stories/2013/12/esc_novels_change_brain/campus.html.

4. Mac History, "1984 Apple's Macintosh Commercial," YouTube video, 0:59, 2012, https://www.youtube.com/watch?v=VtvjbmoDx-I.

CHAPTER 11

1. Mayer, David, and Herbert M. Greenberg. "What Makes a Good Salesman." *Harvard Business Review*, July 2006. https://hbr.org/2006/07/what-makes-a-good-salesman.

APPENDIX B

1. Richard, Skip. "Saving Face: How to Preserve Dignity and Build Trust." Skip Prichard | Leadership Insights, June 16, 2020. https://www.skipprichard.com/saving-face-how-to-preserve-dignity-and-build-trust/.

About the Authors

Tina Kuhn is an accomplished CEO with expertise in organizational transformation. She has demonstrated success supporting government agencies and commercial industries.

Her experience spans executive management, operations management, business growth, and project management. Throughout her executive career, Tina has held many leadership positions. At present, she serves as President and CEO of a cyber security company.

Tina holds a Bachelor of Science degree in Information Systems Management from the University of Maryland. Additionally, she earned her Project Management Professional (PMP) credentials through the Project Management Institute (PMI). Tina loves cooking, running, and watching British detective shows.

Tina's book, *The Manager's Communication Tool Kit: Tools and Techniques for Leading Difficult Personalities*, is a clear and practical guide to high-performance business communication.

Neal Frick is a CEO with more than twenty years of experience in organizational growth and development.

Neal's experience spans talent acquisition leadership, operations management, business growth, human resources leadership, and growing start-ups. Throughout his career, he has held several executive leadership positions and currently serves as CEO of a company supporting the United States Intelligence Community.

He is an unapologetic nerd whose passion for improving the work environments of his team members is matched only by his passion for overdramatic sci-fi movies.